CW00357957

Design Considerations for Datacom Equipment Centers

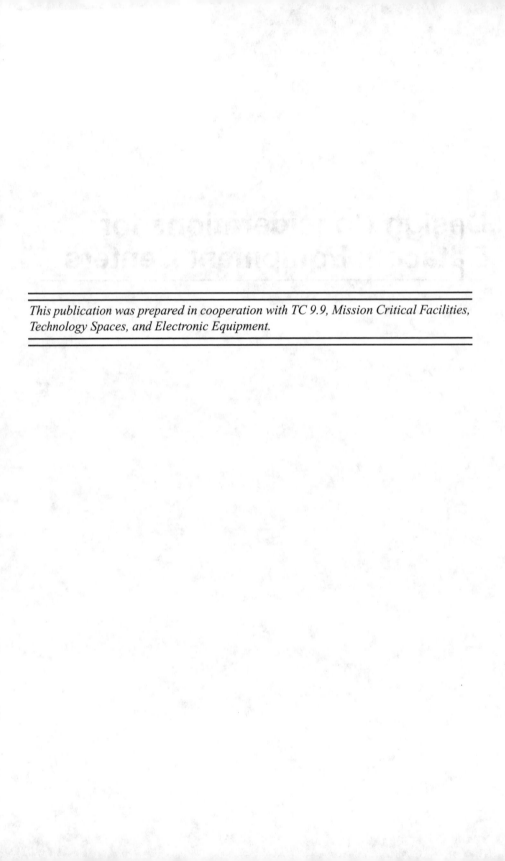

This publication was prepared in cooperation with TC 9.9, Mission Critical Facilities, Technology Spaces, and Electronic Equipment.

Design Considerations for Datacom Equipment Centers

American Society of Heating, Refrigerating and Air-Conditioning Engineers, Inc.

ISBN 1-931862-94-X   ISBN 13 978-1-931862-94-3

©2005 American Society of Heating, Refrigerating
and Air-Conditioning Engineers, Inc.
1791 Tullie Circle, NE
Atlanta, GA 30329
www.ashrae.org

All rights reserved.

Printed in the United States of America

ASHRAE has compiled this publication with care, but ASHRAE has not investigated, and ASHRAE expressly disclaims any duty to investigate, any product, service, process, procedure, design, or the like that may be described herein. The appearance of any technical data or editorial material in this publication does not constitute endorsement, warranty, or guaranty by ASHRAE of any product, service, process, procedure, design, or the like. ASHRAE does not warrant that the information in the publication is free of errors, and ASHRAE does not necessarily agree with any statement or opinion in this publication. The entire risk of the use of any information in this publication is assumed by the user.

No part of this book may be reproduced without permission in writing from ASHRAE, except by a reviewer who may quote brief passages or reproduce illustrations in a review with appropriate credit; nor may any part of this book be reproduced, stored in a retrieval system, or transmitted in any way or by any means—electronic, photocopying, recording, or other—without permission in writing from ASHRAE.

Design considerations for datacom equipment centers.
     p. cm.
   "This publication was prepared in cooperatiion with TC 9.9, Mission Critical Facilities, Technology Spaces, and Electronic Equipment."
   Includes bibliographical references and index.
   ISBN 1-931862-94-X (pbk.)   ISBN 13 978-1-931862-94-3
   1. Office buildings--Design and construction. 2. Electronic data processing departments--Equipment and supplies--Protection. 3. Telecommunication--Equipment and supplies--Protection. 4. Electronic data processing--Equipment and supplies--Protection. I. American Society of Heating, Refrigerating and Air-Conditioning Engineers. TC 9.9, Mission Critical Facilities, Technology Spaces, and Electronic Equipment.

TH4311.D46 2005
690'.523--dc22
                              2005034568

ASHRAE STAFF

SPECIAL PUBLICATIONS

Mildred Geshwiler
Editor

Christina Helms
Associate Editor

Cindy Sheffield Michaels
Editorial Assistant

Michshell Phillips
Administrative Assistant

PUBLISHING SERVICES

David Soltis
Manager

Tracy Becker
Graphic Applications Specialist

Jayne Jackson
Production Assistant

PUBLISHER

W. Stephen Comstock

Contents

Part II: Other Considerations

viii | **Contents**

Acknowledgments

The information in this guide was produced with the help and support of the corporations listed below.

A.G. Edwards
ANCIS
American Power Conversion
Bell South
Citigroup
Data Aire, Inc.
Dell Computers
Department of Defense NSA
DLB Associates Consulting Engineers
EDS
EYP Mission Critical Facilities
Fannie Mae
Fluent, Inc.
Fujitsu Laboratories of America
Heapy Engineering
Hewlett Packard

IBM
Intel Corporation
Lawrence Berkeley National
    Laboratories
Liebert Corporation
Mallory & Evans, Inc.
Nelson Acoustical
Nortel
Northwest Airlines
Rice University
Stulz-ATS
Sun Microsystems
Syska & Hennessy Group, Inc.
Tier 4 Consulting
Wright Line, LLC

ASHRAE TC 9.9 wishes to particularly thank the following people:

- **David Copeland, Tom Davidson, Dennis Hellmer, Christopher Kurkjian, Budy Notohardjono, Dick Pressley, Joe Prisco, Terry Rodgers, Roger Schmidt, Vali Sorell, Fred Stack, Benjamin Steinberg,** and **Jeff Trower** for their participation as chapter leads, which included numerous conference calls, writing, and review

- **Dr. Roger Schmidt** of IBM for his invaluable participation in the writing and final editing of this book
- **Mr. Tom Davidson** of DLB Associates Consulting Engineers for his editing of multiple drafts of this book
- **Mr. Don Beaty** of DLB Associates Consulting Engineers, chair of TC 9.9, for his vision for this book and for his drive and leadership in turning that vision into a reality.

In addition, ASHRAE TC 9.9 would like to thank the following people for their substantial contributions to the creation of this book: John Adelsberger, Paul Benanti, Mark Germagian, Jack Glass, Andrew Higgins, Magnus Herrlin, Kishor Khankari, Matt Lawrence, Bret Lehman, Renee Marzitelli, David Nelson, Matthew Nobile, Ron Shapiro, Bella Treyger, William Tschudi, and Jim VanGilder.

1

Introduction

Datacom (data processing and telecommunications) facilities are predominantly populated with computers, networking equipment, electronic equipment, and peripherals. The most defining HVAC characteristic of data and communications equipment centers is the potential for exceptionally high heat loads—often orders of magnitude greater than in a typical office building.

In addition, the equipment installed in these facilities typically:

- *Serves mission critical applications* (i.e., continuous operation 7 days × 24 hours). The potential consequences of downtime to the enterprise must be thoroughly examined by all interested parties from as early in the design of the project as possible. Single points of failure must be addressed from a design standpoint so that they can be identified and eliminated.
- *Has special environmental requirements* (temperature, humidity, and cleanliness). The need to provide high reliability means that careful attention must be given to maintenance of appropriate temperature, humidity, and cleanliness criteria. This will be discussed in great detail throughout the publication but is particularly and specifically covered in chapter 2, "Design Criteria," where the Class 1-Class 4 and NEBS classifications of standardized conditions are defined and discussed.
- *Has the potential for overheating and resultant equipment failure due to a sudden loss of cooling.* Thermal failure of compute equipment and hardware is only one manifestation of the risk associated with high temperatures and lack of environmental control. Shortened life span of electronic equipment and intermittent failures of the datacom equipment with disruption to the enterprise, failure to maintain service level agreements (SLA), and subsequent costs are additional considerations.

The design of any datacom facility should also address the fact that most datacom equipment will be replaced one or more times during the life of the facility with more current technology. As described in ASHRAE's *Datacom Equipment Power*

Trends and Applications (ASHRAE 2005i), typical datacom equipment product cycles are 1 to 5 years, whereas the datacom facility that houses this equipment and the HVAC equipment and infrastructure have life cycles that could be anywhere from 10 to 25 years. Replacement equipment has historically required more demanding power and cooling requirements.

In addition to replacement of datacom equipment over the life of the facility, there is a continual need to upgrade individual computer devices, which will probably result in a change in the heat load and a change in the needs for air distribution. To the extent that changes can be planned for or otherwise accommodated during the life of the electronic space, careful consideration must be given by all potentially impacted stakeholders as to how these additions and modifications might take place.

It may also be necessary to plan for future physical expansion and increases in both localized and overall watt density. This may include headers, conduits, and other infrastructure provisions to accommodate equipment in a plug and play fashion over the useful life of the facility.

Understanding the critical parameters outlined above is essential to facility design in this environment. The intended audience for this document is:

- Planners and managers planning a datacom facility
- Datacom facility design teams planning and designing a datacom facility
- Datacom facility architects and engineers who require insight on datacom equipment energy density and installation planning trends.

OVERVIEW OF CHAPTERS

Chapter 1, Introduction. The introduction states the purpose/objective of the document as well as a brief overview of the upcoming chapters.

Part I: Datacom Facility Basics

The intent of Part I of this book is to provide basic information essential for the design of datacom facilities. It covers the topics of design criteria, HVAC loads, cooling systems overview, air distribution, and liquid cooling.

Chapter 2, Design Criteria. The chapter describes the standards for manufacturer classifications of datacom equipment and then, based on these classifications, provides environmental design criteria for equipment. Temperature, temperature rate of change, humidity, filtration/contamination, ventilation, envelope considerations, human comfort, and flexibility are introduced in a broad sense, with many of these topics expanded upon in greater detail elsewhere in this publication.

Chapter 3, HVAC Load Considerations. While the methodologies for determining heat loads of electronic spaces can be much the same as for other types of areas with cooling requirements, the critical nature of the space, combined with the typically high heat generating equipment in the space, makes the task more difficult. Infrastructure equipment such as power conditioning and power distribution devices, the potential for concentrated loads of high density, and the need for proper air distribution—all make the design challenge that much more formidable and critical.

Chapter 4, Computer Room Cooling Overview. Computer room air conditioners (CRAC), their cooling methodologies, and their location are covered in the first part of this chapter. Central station air handlers and chilled water distribution are also introduced as alternative methods for cooling. The relationship between methods of heat rejection as accomplished by direct expansion versus chilled-water systems is described along with the functional characteristics and interrelationships of the refrigeration cycle, condensers, chillers, pumps, piping, and humidifiers. The chapter concludes with a description of control parameters and monitoring methodologies.

Chapter 5, Air Distribution. Equipment airflow protocol standardization and hot-aisle/cold-aisle configuration are defined in this chapter. Distribution of chilled air to the space, whether via underfloor or overhead methods, is described and discussed in terms of strengths, weaknesses, and certain applications. The effective management of return air is also covered.

Chapter 6, Liquid Cooling. Definitions of air cooling and liquid cooling are followed by an overview of liquid cooling. The liquids that are specifically referenced in this chapter include water, dielectric fluids, and refrigerants. A discussion of chilled-water systems is followed by a section on reliability.

Part II: Other Considerations

The intent of Part II of this book is to provide information that is supplemental to basic data center design, which may be of more value to those who already have design and/or operating experience in this field. It covers the topics of ancillary spaces, contamination, acoustics, structural and seismic design, fire suppression, commissioning, availability and redundancy, and energy efficiency.

Chapter 7, Ancillary Spaces. Support, infrastructure and ancillary equipment may be placed either inside or outside of the datacom equipment room. In some cases this equipment will generate its own heat load, and it may or may not have environmental requirements comparable to the datacom equipment itself. Battery plants, engine generator rooms, and storage facilities all have their own requirements and may be essential to the mission critical nature of the overall space.

Chapter 8, Contamination. Several categories of contamination, their causes, effects, measurement, and prevention, are covered in this chapter. Classifications include solids, liquids, and gases. Contaminants introduced by fire suppression and air-conditioning equipment, as well as printers, floor and ceiling tiles, and the electronic hardware itself are all referenced and discussed in detail. VOCs and zinc, tin, and iron whiskers, their potential origins and resultant damage, are covered as well. The reader will find references to filter and heat sink clogging, arcing, head crashing and connector failures. The chapter concludes with several tables that refer to ASHRAE, OSHA, military, Belcore/Telcordia, NIOSH, and other standards, measurements, and criteria.

Chapter 9, Acoustical Noise Emissions. The combined trends of increased airflow and an increase in the number of people physically present and working in the datacom room make noise levels an area of concern. ASHRAE references, descriptions of source, path, and receiver, effects on people, and definitions of sound power and sound pressure are detailed. The role of regulatory agencies and the potential problems caused by excessive noise are further discussed.

Chapter 10, Structural and Seismic. Floor structure, weight distribution, vibration isolation, and floor loading are addressed in this chapter in terms of both structural and seismic considerations. Formulae for calculating floor loads and diagrammatic examples are provided. Access floor panel considerations and the effects of heavy loads concentrated on casters are described. The chapter also makes reference to necessary considerations in earthquake zones.

Chapter 11, Fire Detection and Suppression. Methods of guarding against, preventing, and dealing with smoke and fire in the electronic equipment space are addressed in this chapter of the book. Exhaust systems, smoke dampers, smoke detectors, and various code-related preventive and reactive design and operational related details are discussed. Wet and dry suppression agents and their use and design considerations are covered.

Chapter 12, Commissioning. Most facilities undergo some degree of commissioning as part of the owner's acceptance process. This chapter details the five steps of formal commissioning activities, starting with the facility's intent and performance requirements (as determined by the project team) and following with the Owner's Program document, Basis of Design document, and the project commissioning plan. These activities include factory acceptance tests, field component verification, system construction verification, site acceptance testing, and integrated systems testing. The role of building automation systems is also discussed, along with commissioning costs based on the various levels of commissioning.

Chapter 13, Availability and Redundancy. In a 24×7×365 facility, availability and redundancy should be given extremely serious consideration. This chapter details aspects of availability such as the concept of five 9's, failure prediction, mean time between failure, and mean time to repair. Concepts of redundancy such as "$N+1$," "$N+2$," and "$2N$" are introduced, defined, and discussed, as well as the use of computational fluid dynamics for determining air distribution under various operational scenarios. Diversity and human error, as well as some practical examples of methods to increase availability and redundancy, are presented.

Chapter 14, Energy Efficiency. The discussion of energy efficiency in this chapter falls into four general categories: environmental criteria, generation, distribution, and "other measures." Specific topics include chilled-water plants, CRAC units, fans, pumps, variable-frequency drives, humidity control, air- and water-side economizers, part-load operation, in-room airflow distribution, and datacom equipment energy efficiency.

The book concludes with a list of references and a glossary of terms.

Part I

Datacom Facility Basics

2

Design Criteria

Datacom facilities that house the following types of datacom equipment require air conditioning to maintain proper environmental conditions:

- High-performance computers
- Storage servers
- Compute servers
- Networking equipment
- Personal computers
- Other rack and cabinet-mounted equipment

Personnel also occupy datacom facilities, but their occupancy is typically transient and environmental conditions are more typically dictated by equipment needs. However, the human occupancy for smaller datacom facilities may influence the ventilation air quantity and quality.

2.1 OVERVIEW

Environmental requirements of datacom equipment may vary depending on the type of equipment and/or manufacturer. However, there has been agreement among a consortium of manufacturers on a set of four standardized conditions (Classes 1- 4). These conditions are listed in the ASHRAE publication *Thermal Guidelines for Data Processing Environments* (ASHRAE, 2004h). An additional classification, the Network Equipment-Building Systems (NEBS) class, is typically used in telecommunications environments. Definitions of all classes are provided below:

- **Class 1**: Typically a datacom facility with tightly controlled environmental parameters (dew point, temperature, and relative humidity) and mission critical operations; types of products typically designed for this environment are enterprise servers and storage products.

- **Class 2**: Typically a datacom space or office or lab environment with some control of environmental parameters (dew point, temperature, and relative humidity); types of products typically designed for this environment are small servers, storage products, personal computers, and workstations.

- **Class 3**: Typically an office, home, or transportable environment with little control of environmental parameters (temperature only); types of products typically designed for this environment are personal computers, workstations, laptops, and printers.

- **Class 4**: Typically a point-of-sale or light industrial or factory environment with weather protection, sufficient winter heating, and ventilation; types of products typically designed for this environment are point-of-sale equipment, ruggedized controllers, or computers and PDAs.

- **NEBS**: According to Telcordia GR-63-CORE (Issue 2, April 2002) and GR-3028-CORE (Issue 1, December 2001), typically a telecommunications central office with some control of environmental parameters (dew point, temperature, and relative humidity): types of products typically designed for this environment are switches, transport equipment, and routers.

- Since Class 3 and 4 environments are not designed primarily for the datacom equipment, they are not covered further in this chapter, and reference should be made to ASHRAE's *Thermal Guidelines* book for further information (ASHRAE 2004h).

2.2   ENVIRONMENTAL REQUIREMENTS

Table 2.1 lists the recommended and allowable conditions for the Class 1, Class 2, and NEBS environments as defined by the sources that are footnoted. Figure 2.1a shows recommended temperature and humidity conditions for Class 1, Class 2, and NEBS classes on a psychrometric chart. Figure 2.1b shows allowable temperature and humidity conditions for the same classes. It should be noted that the dew-point temperature is also specified, as well as the relative humidity.

An additional parameter that affects the ability of datacom equipment to be adequately cooled is air density. ASHRAE's *Thermal Guidelines for Data Processing Environments* (ASHRAE 2004h) suggests that data center products be designed to operate up to 10,000 ft (3050 m) altitude, but it recognizes that there is reduced mass flow and convective heat transfer associated with lower air density at higher elevations. To account for this effect, the guideline includes a de-rating chart for the maximum allowable temperature of 1°F/550 ft altitude above 2950 ft (1°C/300 m altitude above 900 m). Figure 2.2 shows the de-rating recommended by *Thermal Guidelines* for Classes 1and 2 and for NEBS.

The stated environmental conditions are as measured at the inlet to the data and communications equipment and not average space or return air conditions.

Table 2.1 Class 1, Class 2, and NEBS Design Conditions

Condition	Class 1 / Class 2		NEBS	
	Allowable Level	Recommended Level	Allowable Level	Recommended Level
Temperature control range	59°F-90°F[a,f] (Class 1) 50°F-95°F[a,f] (Class 2)	68°F-77°F[a]	41°F-104°F[c,f]	65°F-80°F[d]
Maximum temperature rate of change	9°F per hour[a]		2.9°F/min. [d]	
Relative humidity control range	20%-80% 63°F. Max Dew point[a] (Class 1) 70°F. Max Dew point[a] (Class 2)	40%-55%[a]	5%-85% 82°F Max Dew point[c]	Max 55%[e]
Filtration quality	65%, min. 30%[b] (MERV 11, min. MERV 8)[b]			

[a]These conditions are inlet conditions recommended in the ASHRAE Publication *Thermal Guidelines for Data Processing Environments* (ASHRAE, 2004h). Metric equivalents can be found in that publication.
[b]Percentage values in accord with ASHRAE Standard 52.1 (ASHRAE 1992) dust-spot efficiency test. MERV values according to ASHRAE Standard 52.2 (ASHRAE 1999). Refer to Table 8.4 of this publication for the correspondence between MERV, ASHRAE 52.1 and ASHRAE 52.2 Filtration Standards.
[c]Telcordia 2002 GR-63-CORE
[d]Telcordia 2001 GR-3028-CORE
[e]Generally accepted telecom practice. Telecom central offices are not generally humidified, but grounding of personnel is common practice to reduce ESD.
[f]Refer to Figure 2.2 for temperature de-rating with altitude

2.3 TEMPERATURE

Equipment exposed to high temperature, or to high thermal gradients, can experience thermal failure, particularly when repeatedly exposed to such high thermal gradients. Manufacturer's specifications for inlet air conditions to datacom equipment should always be checked, but a typical recommended range is 68°F to 77°F (20°C-25°C). For telecommunications central offices and NEBS, the ranges are wider (Table 2.1). The recommended range of 65°F to 80°F (18°C-27°C) in GR-3028-CORE is based on an economic analysis (Herrlin 1996), including:

- Energy costs associated with operating the HVAC system
- Battery replacement costs
- Datacom equipment repair
- Cleaning costs

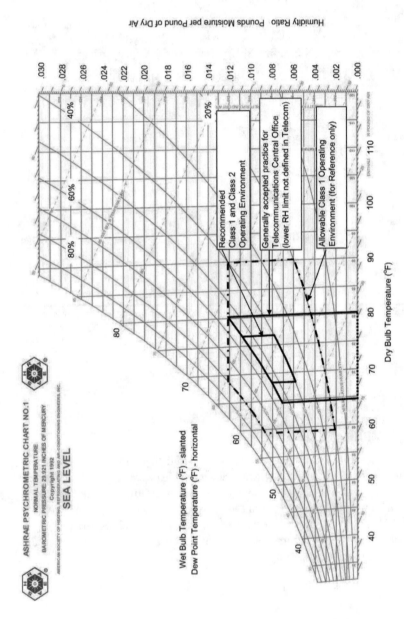

Figure 2.1a Recommended data center Class 1, Class 2, and NEBS operating conditions. Refer to ASHRAE's Thermal Guidelines (ASHRAE 2004h) for an equivalent figure with SI units.

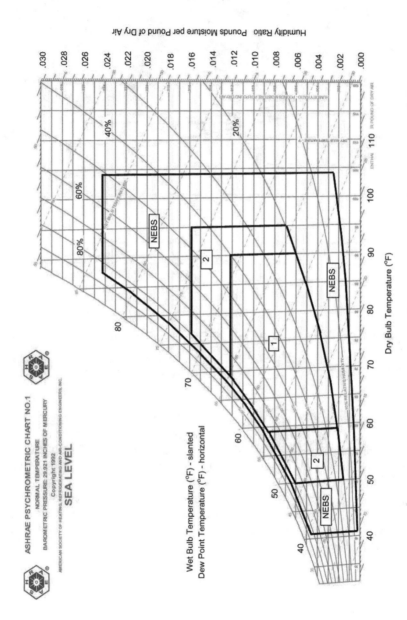

Figure 2.1b Allowable data center Class 1, Class 2, and NEBS operating conditions. Refer to ASHRAE's Thermal Guidelines (ASHRAE 2004h) for an equivalent figure with SI units.

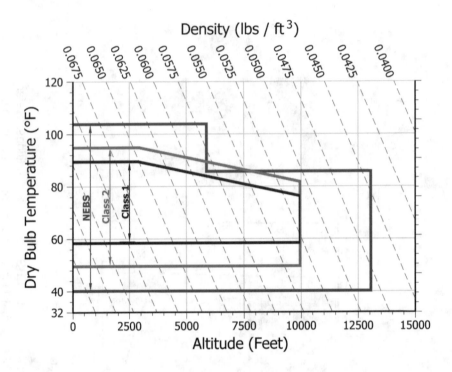

Figure 2.2 Class 1, Class 2, and NEBS allowable temperature range vs. altitude.

Operation in the allowable range should usually be considered as acceptable for short periods of time; however, the longer equipment is operated in the allowable versus the recommended range, the shorter the equipment life will be. Short excursions into or slightly above the allowable range could cause disk failures, data corruption, or CPU lockups. Conversely, the long-term effect of operating in the high end of the allowable range will result in shortened life of the equipment. Always refer to manufacturers' specifications regarding recommended and allowable operating ranges. Facility designers and operators should strive for operation in the recommended range.

2.4   TEMPERATURE RATE OF CHANGE

Some datacom manufacturers have established criteria for allowable rates of environmental change to prevent shock to the data and communications equipment. These criteria need to be reviewed for all installed datacom equipment. A maximum change of 9°F (5°C) per hour is recommended in ASHRAE's *Thermal Guidelines for Data Processing Environments* (ASHRAE 2004h) for Classes 1 and 2. Humidity rate of change is typically most important for tape and storage products. Typical requirements for tape are a rate of change of less than 3.5°F (2°C) per hour and a relative humidity change of less than 5% per hour (ASHRAE 2004h).

In telecommunications central offices, the NEBS requirement in GR-63-CORE for testing of new equipment is a rate change of 54°F (30°C) per hour. However, in the event of an air-conditioning failure, the rate of change in temperature can easily be significantly higher. Consequently, NEBS GR-3028-CORE recommends additional equipment testing with a gradient of 2.9°F/min (1.6°C/min) for 15 minutes. Manufacturer's requirements should be reviewed and fulfilled to ensure that the system will function properly during normal operation and during start-up and shutdown.

Procedures must be in place for response to an event that shuts down critical cooling systems while critical loads continue to operate, as the space will immediately begin increasing in temperature. Procedures should also be in place governing how fast elevated space temperatures can be returned to normal to avoid thermal shock damage.

Datacom equipment usually tolerates a somewhat wider range of environmental conditions when not in use (*Thermal Guidelines for Data Processing Environments* [ASHRAE 2004h], Table 2.1). However, it may be desirable to operate the cooling systems regardless to keep the room within the operating limits and minimize thermal shock to the equipment.

2.5 HUMIDITY

High relative humidity may cause various problems to datacom equipment. Such problems include conductive anodic failures (CAF), hygroscopic dust failures (HDF), tape media errors and excessive wear, and corrosion. In extreme cases, condensation can occur on cold surfaces of direct-cooled equipment. Low relative humidity may result in electrostatic discharge (ESD), which can destroy equipment or adversely affect operation. Tape products and media may have excessive errors when exposed to low relative humidity.

2.6 FILTRATION AND CONTAMINATION

Table 2.1 contains both recommended and minimum allowable filtration guidelines for recirculated air in a data center. Dust can adversely affect the operation of datacom equipment, so high-quality filtration and proper filter maintenance are essential. Corrosive gases can quickly destroy the thin metal film conductors used in printed circuit boards, and corrosion can cause high resistance at terminal connection points. In addition, the accumulation of dust and other contaminants on surfaces needed for heat removal, i.e., heat sink fins, can retard the ability of the heat removal device to perform properly.

Outside air should be treated and preconditioned to remove dust, salts, and corrosive gases before it is introduced into the data and or communications equipment room. One study has shown that a high level of space pressurization can increase dust levels in the facility relative to a low pressurization level, even with outdoor air filters rated at 85% efficiency (MERV 13) (Herrlin 1997). This might point to a need for pre-filters and high filter efficiency final filters for outdoor air or to a decision to maintain a lower pressurization level to reduce contamination through the outdoor air filters. Ambient dust levels may play a part in the choice of filtration efficiency. A potential problem with a low pressurization level is that infiltration can occur at high wind velocity and humidity levels can be adversely affected.

Certain mission critical facilities may wish to reduce contamination from particulates by designing to clean room standards. The primary standard in this area is International Organization for Standardization (ISO) 14644-1 (ISO 1999b). Possible design levels include ISO Class 7 and ISO Class 8. Always adhere to preventive maintenance and standard operating procedures related to filter inspection and replacement.

2.7   VENTILATION

Outside air is introduced to the data center space for one of the following four reasons: to maintain indoor air quality requirements, to pressurize the space to keep contaminants out, as makeup air for smoke purge, or to conserve energy when outside air conditions are conducive to free cooling.

Indoor air quality requirements are spelled out in ASHRAE Standard 62.1-2004 (ASHRAE 2004j). Although not inclusive of all the air quality requirements for datacom environments (see chapter 8 for more details), it helps to ensure that adequate quantity and quality of ventilation air is available to all building occupants.

The data center is pressurized in order to avoid infiltration and to keep out unwanted contaminants such as dust. Chapter 8 of this book covers the topic of contamination in detail. Pressurization calculations can be performed using the procedures outlined in the *2005 ASHRAE Handbook—Fundamentals*, chapter 27, "Ventilation and Infiltration" (ASHRAE 2005e).

Outside air is also necessary as makeup when smoke purge systems are installed. Chapter 11 of this book deals specifically with this issue.

Finally, when outdoor conditions permit, additional outdoor air can be brought into the space to provide "free" cooling. This can reduce the operating cost of the air-conditioning system. Chapter 14 of this book discusses energy efficiency and free cooling in more detail.

Regardless of the reasons outside air is introduced, it will have an impact on the temperature and relative humidity of the datacom environment and, therefore, should be properly conditioned before introduction. The subject of humidity control and humidification is covered in sections 2.5, 3.4.7, 4.1.3, 4.2.2, 4.10, and 14.6.

2.8   ENVELOPE CONSIDERATIONS

There are several parameters that should be considered in designing the envelope of datacom facilities. These parameters include pressurization, isolation, vapor retardants, sealing, and condensation.

- **Pressurization**—Datacom facilities are typically pressurized to prevent infiltration of air and pollutants through the building envelope. An air lock is recommended for a datacom equipment room door that opens directly to the outside. Excess pressurization with outdoor air should be avoided, as it makes swinging doors harder to use and wastes energy through increased fan energy and coil loads. Variable-speed outdoor air systems, controlled by differential pressure controllers, are able to ramp up to minimize infiltration and may be a good control strategy.
- **Space Isolation**—Datacom equipment centers are usually isolated for both security and environmental control.
- **Vapor Retardants**—To maintain proper relative humidity in datacom facilities in otherwise un-humidified spaces, vapor retardants should be installed around the entire envelope. The retardant should be sufficient to restrain moisture migration during the maximum projected vapor pressure difference between datacom equipment room and the surrounding areas.
- **Sealing**—Cable and pipe entrances should be sealed and caulked with a fireproof vapor-retarding material. Door jambs should fit tightly.
- **Condensation on Exterior Glazing**—For exterior walls in colder climates, windows should be double or triple glazed and door seals specified to prevent condensation and infiltration. Many datacom facilities are designed or retrofitted without windows in humidified areas to avoid the condensation problem.

2.9   HUMAN COMFORT

Human comfort is not specifically addressed in *Thermal Guidelines for Data Processing Environments* (ASHRAE 2004h) because such facilities typically have minimal and transient human occupancy. Although telecommunications central offices often have permanent staff working on the equipment, human comfort is not the main objective. Following the recommended Class 1 conditions (Table 2.1) in a hot-aisle/cold-aisle configuration may result in comfort conditions that are cold in the cold aisle and warm or even hot in the hot aisle. Personnel that work in these spaces need to consider the temperature gradient that exists and dress accordingly. If the hot aisle is excessively hot, provisions should be made for providing portable spot cooling. The National Institute for Occupational Safety and Health (NIOSH) provides detailed guidance on occupational exposure to hot environments (NIOSH 1986). Another concern is contact burns if equipment is too hot. Human tissue reaches the pain threshold at 111°F (44°C), and various levels of injury occur at levels above 111°F (44°C) (ASTM 2003). Care should be taken that equipment surface temperatures do not represent a hazard. Further guidance on surface temperatures that produce burn injuries is available from ASTM (2003).

2.10 FLEXIBILITY

As described in the opening, technology is continually changing and therefore datacom equipment in a given space is frequently changed and /or rearranged during the life of a datacom facility. As a result, the HVAC system serving the facility must be sufficiently flexible to permit "plug and play" rearrangement of components and expansion without excessive disruption of the production environment. In critical applications, it should be possible to modify the system without shutdown. If possible, the cooling system should be modular and designed to efficiently handle a wide range of heat loads.

2.11 ADDITIONAL CONSIDERATIONS

When designing or selecting datacom air-conditioning equipment, the following should also be considered:

- Type of system
     Air cooled
     Glycol cooled
     Water cooled
     Refrigerant cooled
     Chilled water
     Dual source
- Cooling load, including breakdown of the load into sensible and latent components
- Entering and leaving dry-bulb/wet-bulb temperatures and relative humidity
- Altitude
- In the case of chilled water—flow rate, entering and leaving water temperatures, pressure drop
- Airflow rates through cooling equipment and IT equipment
- Distribution and balancing of airflow (or other cooling medium)

3

HVAC Load Considerations

HVAC loads in datacom facilities must be calculated in the same manner as for any other facility. Typical features of these facilities are a high internal sensible heat load from the datacom equipment itself and a correspondingly high sensible heat ratio. However, other loads exist and it is important that a composite load composed of all sources be calculated early in the design phase, rather than relying on a generic overall "watts per square foot" estimate that neglects other potentially important loads.

Also, if the initial deployment or "Day 1" datacom equipment load is low due to low equipment occupancy, the impact of the other loads (envelope, lighting, etc.) becomes proportionately more important in terms of part-load operation.

3.1   DATACOM EQUIPMENT

The major heat source in datacom facilities is the datacom equipment itself. This heat can be highly concentrated, not uniformly distributed, and variable. Equipment that generates large quantities of heat is normally configured with internal fans and airflow passages to transport the cooling air, usually drawn from the space, through the specific piece of equipment.

Information on datacom equipment heat release should be obtained from the manufacturer. The ASHRAE publication *Thermal Guidelines for Data Processing Environments* (ASHRAE 2004h) includes a sample "Equipment Thermal Report" that, if utilized, should provide heat release information in a format that is specifically suited for thermal design purposes. Nameplate information for data and communications equipment should not be used for thermal design purposes, as it will yield unrealistically high design values and an oversized cooling system infrastructure.

Most datacom equipment manufactured today has variable airflow cooling fans that are dependent on inlet temperature and/or load. Under typical operating conditions, the flow requirements of these fans may be low, but they will increase as the

CPU becomes more highly utilized and/or under extreme conditions such as high system inlet temperature. Consideration of this variable flow may be important to HVAC system design.

3.2   EQUIPMENT LOADS, INCLUDING HIGH-DENSITY LOADS

3.2.1   Trends

The predominant cooling load in almost all datacom facilities is the sensible datacom equipment load. At the time of this writing, the heat density of certain types of datacom equipment is increasing dramatically. Stand-alone server heat loads (or rack loads) have increased to over 30 kW per rack. Such dramatic changes require a design engineer to keep abreast of the latest design techniques to ensure adequate cooling for current loads and flexibility to adapt to the changes caused by future equipment deployments.

Caution should be exercised to ensure that even a single rack with a high-density heat load is provided adequate cooling in a localized sense, even if the overall heat density of the general space is below the "high density" threshold. Rack inlet conditions should be checked and verified as adequate to meet the manufacturer's requirements. Refer to ASHRAE's *Thermal Guidelines for Data Processing Environments* (ASHRAE 2004h) for additional information and guidance.

With the increase in heat density, we are approaching the upper limits of air-cooled solutions. In response, there is an increased interest in more efficient cooling techniques, such as liquid cooling of the cabinets and in some cases the electronics. The liquid cooling media might consist of water, refrigerants, high dielectric fluorocarbons, or two-phase fluids such as dielectrics. Some manufacturers have already taken this approach. The reader is encouraged to keep abreast of research and development in this area.

New datacom facilities and those slated for major renovation should consider adding appropriate infrastructure (piping taps, feeders, etc.) for future use and load increases. These "backbones" are typically much more expensive, disruptive, and risky to retrofit within an existing operating environment.

3.2.2   Equipment Heat Load Calculations

Calculation of the datacom heat load density in a facility for design purposes is a moving target. It is one of the primary reasons for publication of *Datacom Equipment Power Trends and Cooling Applications* (ASHRAE 2005i). To determine the design heat load in a facility based on data in the *Power Trends* book, it is necessary to (a) define a target design date for the facility (since loads are projected to increase at least through the year 2014) and (b) to know the approximate datacom facility area breakdown by type of datacom equipment or other use.

Types of equipment are broken down in *Datacom Equipment Power Trends and Cooling Applications* into seven categories.

- Tape storage
- Workstations (stand-alone)
- Storage servers
- Compute servers – 2U and greater
- Compute servers – 1U, blade, and custom
- Communication – high density
- Communication – extreme density

Once the percentage breakdown of each type of equipment in a space is known, the number of square feet of each type of equipment could be estimated as:

Equipment Type xx = x% of floor area × Overall Area = X square feet,
Equipment Type yy = y% of floor area × Overall Area = Y square feet, etc.

The overall heat load can then be estimated by multiplying the heat density of each type of equipment by the floor areas of this type of equipment and then summing the various types of equipment. Table 3.1 has a sample calculation for a facility being designed to handle heat loads to be expected by datacom equipment installed in the year 2005.

While only a sample calculation, the example shows that high-density data centers can be a reality with existing datacom equipment.

3.3   ELECTRICAL DISTRIBUTION EQUIPMENT

In some cases, power distribution units (PDUs) are located in the datacom equipment room as the final means of transforming voltage to a usable rating and distributing power to the datacom equipment. The heat dissipation from the transformers that are contained within these PDUs should be accounted for by referencing the manufacturer's equipment specifications. If uninterruptible power supply (UPS) units are located in the datacom equipment room, the heat generated by this equipment must also be taken into consideration.

3.4   OTHER LOADS

3.4.1   Ventilation and Infiltration

For load calculation protocols relating to ventilation and infiltration, refer to chapter 27, "Ventilation and Infiltration," of the *2005 ASHRAE Handbook—Fundamentals* (ASHRAE 2005e).

The outdoor air requirements of datacom facilities may be lower than other facilities due to the light human occupancy load. In many cases, it is advantageous to precondition this air (filtration and humidity control) and maintain the datacom space under positive pressure, to allow for 100% sensible cooling in the space.

Table 3.1   Sample Calculation—Overall Heat Loads Expected in a New Facility with Vintage 2005 Equipment

Type of Equipment	Percentage of Raised Floor Space[1]	Total Area (Equipment Footprint)[2] (ft^2)	Density (W/ft^2 of Equipment Footprint), 2005 baseline[3]	Equipment Load (W)
Tape storage	10	1000	175	175,000
Workstations	2	200	660	132,000
Storage servers	10	1000	1125	1,125,000
Compute servers - 2U and greater	5	500	2150	1,075,000
Compute servers - 1U, blade, and custom	1	100	3800	380,000
Communication– high-density	1	100	2600	260,000
Communication– extreme density	1	100	6250	625,000
Aisle space, other uses[4]	70	7000	calculate based actual equipment	35,000
Total	**100**	**10,000**		**3,807,000**
Overage "raised floor" load (W/ft^2)[5]				381

[1] Sample data only, actual values are application specific
[2] Based on a "Raised Floor" area of 10,000 ft^2 (929 m^2)
[3] Density values taken from Table B-1 of ASHRAE's *Power Trends* (ASHRAE, 2005i)
[4] Assumed value; actual value should be calculated with a similar matrix procedure once the usage breakdown of all other areas is identified.
[5] This total is for equipment on the raised floor only. It does not include loads mentioned in Section 3.4

3.4.2   Lights

Heat gain from lights should be determined from the lighting plan. Lighting loads are typically at least an order of magnitude less than datacom equipment loads yet could be reduced through the use of lighting controls, since datacom spaces are often unoccupied.

3.4.3   People

Occupancy loads should be considered as light work. People often compose the only internal latent load in a datacom facility, which may be a factor in the selection of cooling coils.

3.4.4   Envelope

Heat gains through the structure depend on the location and construction of the envelope. If possible, external walls should be avoided. As a minimum, windows should be avoided to minimize sun loading and potential condensation, as well as to allow for increased wall insulation. Special attention should be given to a vapor barrier to minimize the ingress of latent load. More detailed design information on lighting, personnel, and envelope cooling loads can be obtained from the *2005 ASHRAE Handbook—Fundamentals*, chapter 30, "Nonresidential Cooling and Heating Load Calculation Procedures" (ASHRAE 2005f).

3.4.5   Transmission

Although the internal heat gain dominates most data and communication equipment rooms, transmission heat gain to the space should be carefully evaluated and provided for in the design. Refer to chapter 31, "Fenestration," of the *2005 ASHRAE Handbook—Fundamentals*, for additional design information (ASHRAE 2005g).

3.4.6   Heating and Reheat

The need for heat in electronic equipment-loaded portions of datacom facilities is typically minimal, due to the high internal heat gains in the spaces. Still, the initial or "Day 1" loads in many datacom facilities can be low due to low equipment occupancy, so sufficient heating capacity to offset the outdoor air and envelope losses should be included in the design.

Many computer room air-conditioning (CRAC) units include reheat coils for use during the dehumidification process. Reheat during this process must be carefully monitored, and possibly disabled, as simultaneous heating and cooling wastes energy.

3.4.7   Humidification

Humidification and/or dehumidification will be needed in most environments to meet both the recommended (40%-55%) and allowable (20%-80%) relative humidity ranges specified for Class 1 and Class 2 data centers in *Thermal Guidelines for Data Processing Environments* (ASHRAE 2004h).

In most cases the predominant moisture load will be the outdoor air, but all potential loads should be considered. A generally accepted telecom practice is not to provide active humidification for central offices. Instead, personnel grounding practices are typically utilized to minimize electrostatic discharge (ESD) failures.

Vapor retardant analyses should also be performed where humidity-controlled spaces contain outside walls or ceilings. Refer to chapter 25, "Thermal and Water Vapor Transmission Data," of the *2005 ASHRAE Handbook—Fundamentals*, for additional design information (ASHRAE 2005d).

4

Computer Room Cooling Overview

It may be desirable for HVAC systems serving datacom facilities to be independent of other systems in the building, although cross-connection with other systems may be desirable for backup. Redundant air-handling equipment is frequently used, normally with automatic operation. A complete air-handling system should provide ventilation air, air filtration, cooling and dehumidification, humidification, and heating. Refrigeration systems should be independent of other systems and may be required year-round, depending on design.

Datacom equipment rooms can be conditioned with a wide variety of systems, including packaged computer room air-conditioning (CRAC) units and central station air-handling systems. Air-handling and refrigeration equipment may be located either inside or outside datacom equipment rooms.

4.1 COMPUTER ROOM AIR-CONDITIONING (CRAC) UNITS

Computer room air-conditioning (CRAC) units are the most popular datacom cooling solution. CRAC units are specifically designed for datacom equipment room applications and should be built and tested in accordance with the requirements of the latest revision of ANSI/ASHRAE Standard 127, *Method of Testing for Rating Computer and Data Processing Room Unitary Air-Conditioners*.

4.1.1 Cooling

CRAC units are available in several types of cooling system configurations, including chilled water, direct expansion air cooled, direct expansion water cooled, and direct expansion glycol cooled. The direct expansion (DX) units typically have multiple refrigerant compressors with separate refrigeration circuits, air filters, humidifiers, and integrated control systems with remote monitoring panels and interfaces. Reheat coils are an option. CRAC units may also be equipped with propylene glycol precooling coils and associated drycoolers to permit water-side economizer operation where weather conditions make this strategy economical. CRAC units with chilled-water coils may also be fitted with DX coils connected to remote outdoor air-cooled condensing units for redundant cooling sources.

CRAC units utilizing chilled water for cooling do not contain refrigeration equipment within their packaging and generally require less servicing, can be more efficient, provide smaller room temperature variations, and more readily support heat recovery strategies than the equivalent DX equipment.

4.1.2 Location

CRAC units are usually located within the datacom equipment room but may also be remotely located and ducted to the conditioned space. Whether they are remote or not, their temperature and humidity sensors should be located to properly control the inlet air conditions to the datacom equipment within specified tolerances (Table 2.1). Analysis of airflow patterns within the datacom equipment room with advanced techniques such as computational fluid dynamics (CFD) may be required to optimally locate the datacom equipment, the CRAC units, and the corresponding temperature and humidity sensors. Otherwise, it may be possible that the sensors are in a location that is not conditioned by the CRAC unit they control or in a location that is not optimum and thereby forces the cooling system to expend more energy than required.

4.1.3 Humidity Control

Types of available humidifiers within CRAC units may include steam, infrared, and ultrasonic. Thought should be given to maintenance and reliability of humidifiers. It may be beneficial to relocate all humidification to a dedicated central system. Another consideration is that certain humidification methods, or use of improperly treated makeup water, are more likely to carry fine particulates to the space.

Reheat is sometimes used in the dehumidification mode when the air is over-cooled for the purpose of removing moisture. Sensible heat is introduced to supplement the actual load in the space typically by use of electric, hot water, or steam coils upon a call for reheat. Use of waste heat of compression (hot gas) for reheat may also be available as an energy-saving option. Datacom facilities should be enclosed with a vapor barrier for humidity control.

4.1.4 Ventilation

In systems using CRAC units, it may be advantageous to introduce outside air through a dedicated system serving all areas. This dedicated system will often provide pressurization control and also control the humidity in the datacom equipment room based on dew point, allowing the primary system serving the space to provide sensible-only cooling. Figure 4.1 shows an independent outdoor air pre-conditioning system in conjunction with a sensible-only recirculation system.

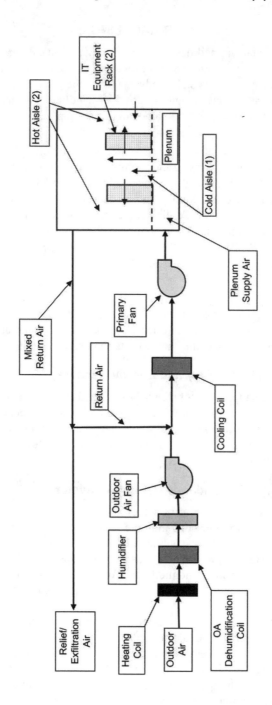

Figure 4.1 Datacom facility with dedicated outdoor air preconditioning.

4.2   CENTRAL STATION AIR-HANDLING UNITS

Some larger datacom facilities use central station air-handling units. Specifically, many telecommunications central offices, regardless of size, utilize central systems. There are advantages and disadvantages to the use of central station air-handling units. Some aspects of central station air-handling units, as they relate to datacom facility applications, are contained in this section.

4.2.1   Coil Selection

There is a wide range of heating and cooling coil types that can be used for datacom facilities and ideally any coil design/specification should include modulating control. In addition, for dehumidification purposes, cooling coils with close dewpoint control is very important. Cooling coil control valves should be designed to "fail open." For more information on cooling coil design, a good reference is the *2004 ASHRAE Handbook—HVAC Systems and Equipment*, chapter 21, "Air-Cooling and Dehumidifying Coils" (ASHRAE 2004e).

4.2.2   Humidification

Central station humidification systems used for datacom facility applications can be of various types. Since humidification costs can be significant, analysis of operating costs using site-specific energy costs should be made (Herrlin 1996).

4.2.3   Part-Load Efficiency and Energy Recovery

Central station supply systems should be designed to accommodate a full range of loads in datacom equipment areas with good part-load efficiency. Due to their larger capacity, central station supply systems may be able to provide more efficient energy recovery options than CRAC units; use of rotary heat exchangers or cross-connected coils should be considered.

4.2.4   Flexibility/Redundancy Using VAV Systems

Flexibility and redundancy can be achieved by using variable-volume air distribution, oversizing, cross-connecting multiple systems, or providing standby equipment. Compared to constant-air-volume units (CAV), variable-air-volume (VAV) equipment can be sized to provide excess capacity but operate at discharge temperatures appropriate for optimum humidity control, minimize operational fan horsepower requirements, provide superior control over space temperature, and reduce the need for reheat.

Common pitfalls of VAV, such as a shift in underfloor pressure distribution and associated flow through tiles, should be modeled using CFD or other analytical techniques to ensure that the system can modulate without adversely affecting overall airflow and cooling capability to critical areas. Variable airflow strategies need to take into consideration the need to get sufficient static pressure to the most limiting rack when operating at minimum flow.

4.3 LIQUID COOLING

High-density racks and other types of datacom equipment referenced in chapter 3 (3.2) may be beyond the upper limits of air-cooled solutions. New datacom equipment is becoming available with liquid cooling in either open architecture or closed architecture configurations. The open architecture systems utilize cooling coils near the heat load, either inside or outside the server rack, and utilize the room air volume as a thermal storage to ride through short power outages. The closed architectures fully enclose the rack with the cooling coil inside. Other provisions are required for power loss ride-through.

The objective of the liquid-cooled systems is to transport the heat away from the datacom equipment. In some configurations, freestanding heat exchangers use the data center's chilled water to cool a separate secondary-loop liquid system, which is connected to the heat exchangers in the data center or integrated into individual equipment racks using an independent pump and piping system. The liquids utilized include water, high dielectric fluids, or refrigerants. The advantage of water is the cost of the fluid, while the disadvantage is the need to address the electric hazard in the event of a leak. The advantage of the high dielectric fluid is that it is nonconductive, while its disadvantages include its high cost and the need for larger pumps and piping systems due to reduced thermal transfer characteristics. The refrigerant solution is a two-phase solution that leaks as a gas—thus, no cleanup or electric hazard. Utilizing the phase change to absorb heat also makes the system more efficient and requires smaller pumping and piping systems verses the water solution. The disadvantages are the fluid cost, the piping installation costs, and the existence of hydrofluorocarbons (HFCs). The desired design with any of these techniques is to maintain the cooling liquid above the dew point. These configurations typically utilize small pipes and flexible hoses with drip-free connect couplings to deliver the warmer chilled water or other liquid to the datacom equipment heat exchangers. These heat exchangers will then return the warmer liquid back to the chilled-water heat exchanger. The supplemental liquid cooling system may utilize cleaner liquid than the standard chilled-water system and include cleanable strainers; operating pressure should be as low as practicable.

Depending on the liquid used, the location of the support mechanical equipment and routing of the piping must coordinate with the "day-one" and future datacom equipment to prevent potential contact between liquid leaks and electronics. Containment of leaks with drip pans and use of leak detectors that could shut down makeup water supply are to be considered and included in the design layouts.

Design of the "day-one" layout and operation should take into account the increasing necessity for future liquid cooling of datacom equipment. The design should include capped connections with isolation valves to accommodate future systems to support developing datacom racks, etc., dependent on liquid cooling.

Additional information on liquid cooling can also be found in chapter 6 of this book and in an *ASHRAE Journal* article (Beaty 2004b).

4.4 CHILLED-WATER DISTRIBUTION SYSTEMS

Chilled-water distribution systems should be designed to the same standards of quality, reliability, and flexibility as other computer room support systems. Where growth is likely, the chilled-water system should be designed for expansion or addition of new equipment without extensive shutdown. Dual sets of risers from the central plant should be considered to allow for a fully fault-tolerant, concurrently maintainable system. Figure 4.2 illustrates a looped chilled-water system with sectional valves and multiple valved branch connections. The branches could serve air handlers or water-cooled computer equipment.

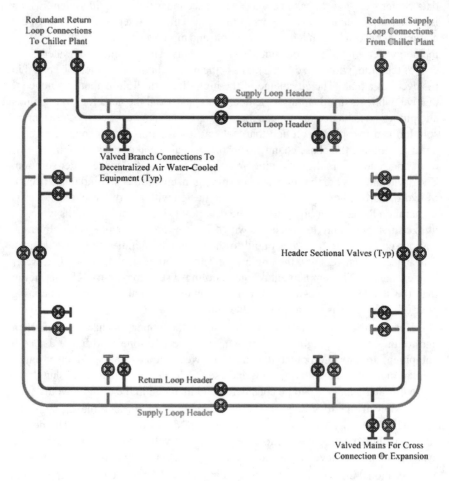

Figure 4.2   Chilled-water loop distribution.

The valve quantity and locations permit modifications or repairs without complete shutdown because chilled water can be fed from either side of the loop. This loop arrangement is a practical method of improving the reliability of a chilled-water system serving a computer room. "Future taps" should have blank flanges with a pressure gauge and drain between the flange and isolation valve to allow the valve to be exercised and checked for holding performance. It is also important to consider the impact the location of the piping may have on the airflow distribution if it is located under the raised floor (see chapter 5.)

Where chilled water serves packaged equipment located in the datacom equipment room, consideration should be given to selecting water temperatures that satisfy the space sensible cooling loads while minimizing the risk of excessive condensation. Since datacom equipment room loads are primarily sensible, chilled water can be relatively warm. Using lower-temperature chilled water, however, will allow for a reduction in chilled water flow that will translate into savings in reduced pump energy and piping installed costs.

However, excessively cold water can result in coil face temperatures below dew point, which can cause unintentional dehumidification and unnecessary humidifier operation and thereby wasted energy. An optimal balance should be found between the reduced operating and installed costs associated with the lower supply temperature and the reduced chiller energy associated with the production of warmer chilled water.

In some facilities, there may be a need for two or more chilled-water temperatures. This could be accomplished with multiple chillers or through the use of an additional heat exchanger to supply warmer chilled water for the uses that require it.

4.5   CONDENSER SYSTEMS

Heat rejection in datacom facilities can be with either water-cooled or air-cooled systems. Basic information on condenser water systems can be obtained from the *2004 ASHRAE Handbook—HVAC Systems and Equipment*, chapter 13, "Condenser Water Systems" (ASHRAE 2004b). Where open cell cooling towers or evaporative cooling is used, consideration should be given to makeup water storage as a backup to the domestic water supply providing condenser water makeup. Also, where an open cooling tower is used, a heat exchanger should be considered to isolate the open water loop from a closed loop supplying the CRAC units to limit the possibility of fouling issues, with the CRAC unit condensers causing increased maintenance at each unit. Alternatively, a cleanable condenser system could be incorporated into the CRAC unit. If this method is utilized and the cooling tower fluid loop is also used to feed a free cooling coil during cooler ambient, the free cooling coil should utilize CuNi piping to minimize the impact contaminants will have on the coil.

Air-cooled systems generally support CRAC units with built-in refrigeration compressors and evaporating coils. These systems consist either of remote air-cooled refrigerant condensers or remote "drycoolers." If remote refrigerant condensers are used, the piping sizes and distances between the compressor and the condenser need to be evaluated to ensure that the refrigerant can travel and still return oil to the compressor. The "drycooler" system incorporates a closed glycol piping loop that transfers heat from a unit-mounted condenser to an outdoor air-to-glycol heat exchanger. When economically feasible, the same glycol loop is sometimes attached to an economizer-cooling coil, installed into the CRAC, which allows for free cooling when the glycol loop temperature is below the return air temperature of the unit.

The greater reliability of air-cooled condensing systems, relative to water-cooled systems, has driven the relative popularity of air-cooled systems for many mission critical facilities. Air-cooled systems also eliminate the need for makeup water systems (and backup makeup water systems). Disadvantages, such as higher operating cost, should be evaluated. Cooling towers, drycoolers, etc., need the same level of redundancy and diversity required of the chillers and other critical infrastructure.

4.6 REFRIGERATION

Refrigeration systems should be designed to match the anticipated cooling load, capable of expansion if necessary, and may be required to provide year-round, continuous operation. Expansion of refrigeration systems while on-line may also be necessary. A separate refrigeration facility for datacom equipment room(s) may be desirable where system requirements differ from those provided for other building and process systems and/or where emergency power requirements preclude combined systems.

Heat recovery chillers may provide an efficient means to recover and reuse heat from datacom equipment environments for comfort heating of typical office environments. The system must provide the reliability and redundancy to match the facility's needs. System operation, servicing, and maintenance should not interfere with facility operation.

4.7 CHILLERS

Since datacom facilities often use large quantities of energy, cooling systems should be designed with the maximum possible efficiency. For large facilities, water-cooled chillers are likely the most efficient system. Basic information on chillers can be obtained from chapter 38, "Liquid Chilling Systems," of the *2004 ASHRAE Handbook—HVAC Systems and Equipment* (ASHRAE 2004f).

Another item to be considered with chiller selection is part-load efficiency, since data centers often operate at less than peak capacity (refer to chapter 14 of this book for more information). The relative energy efficiency of primary versus secondary pumping systems should also be analyzed to optimize energy consumption.

Care must be taken to ensure sectional valves are suitable for bidirectional flow and tight shutoff from flow in either direction to permit maintenance on either side of the valve. In some cases, multiple valves may be required to permit maintenance of the valves themselves.

4.8 PUMPS

Pumps and pumping system design should take into account energy efficiency, reliability, and redundancy. It may be possible to design pumps with variable-speed drives so that the redundant pump is always operational. Ramp-up to full speed occurs on a loss of a given pump.

Basic information on pumps can be obtained from chapter 39, "Centrifugal Pumps," of the *2004 ASHRAE Handbook—HVAC Systems and Equipment* (ASHRAE 2004g). Piping systems are covered in the same volume of the handbook in chapter 12, "Hydronic Heating and Cooling System Design" (ASHRAE 2004a).

4.9 PIPING

Chilled-water and glycol piping must be pressure-tested. The test pressure should be applied in increments to all sections of pipe in the computer area during construction. The piping must also be fully insulated and protected with an effective vapor retardant. Condensate drain lines must also be insulated. Care must be taken during construction in pulling cables underneath a raised floor as it can damage pipe insulation.

It is prudent to provide secondary containment for all piping within datacom equipment rooms. This containment can be either a pan or dammed area under the piping on one end of the cost spectrum or it can be welded, double-containment piping at the other end of the cost spectrum. Secondary containment systems should incorporate leak detection capability. This is not only to detect condensation but also to identify leaks from damaged piping, valves, fittings, etc. In addition, leak detection should also be placed wherever water piping passes through any critical space, regardless of pipe elevation.

Despite this large number of protective measures, telecommunications service providers have historically been reluctant to allow liquid piping in their equipment rooms for cooling purposes. This reluctance, however, has not precluded the presence of other water piping in datacom facilities, such as sprinkler and storm drainage piping (Beaty 2004b).

Piping specialty considerations should include a good quality strainer, with differential pressure alarm, installed to prevent control valve and heat exchanger passages from clogging. Strategically placed drains and vents must be included locally at all equipment. Thermometers and other sensors should be installed in a serviceable manner, as in drywells. Pressure gauges should include gage-cocks.

If cross-connections with other systems are made, possible effects on datacom equipment room systems of the introduction of dirt, scale, or other impurities must be addressed.

Water treatment is an important operational requirement of data center piping systems. Further information can be found in chapter 48, "Water Treatment," of the *2003 ASHRAE Handbook—Applications* (ASHRAE 2003f).

4.10 HUMIDIFIERS

The choice of which humidification technology to use is based on three design characteristics.

1. Water quality (conductivity)
2. System ease of maintenance
3. Energy efficiency

The technology with the widest water quality tolerance is the infrared system, as it has no conductivity requirements. Steam generation is the simplest to maintain via replacement of canister bottles, but this may not be the least expensive depending on the frequency of exchange required (dependent of the mineral content of the water). The most energy efficient is the ultrasonic, provided a supply of deionized water is available. In addition to its low operating cost, ultrasonic humidifiers will help meet the cooling load due to their adiabatic cooling process, which provides approximately 1000 Btu/h (0.3 kWh) of free cooling for every 1 lb/h (0.45 kg/h) of humidification. Note, the cost of deionized water bottles may negate the energy cost savings.

The humidifier must be responsive to control, maintainable, and free of moisture carryover. The humidity sensor should be located to provide control of air inlet conditions to the IT equipment. For additional reference information, chapter 20, "Humidifiers," of the *2004 ASHRAE Handbook—HVAC Systems and Equipment,* is recommended (ASHRAE 2004d).

4.11 CONTROLS AND MONITORING

4.11.1 Controls

Control systems must be capable of reliable control of temperature, relative humidity, and, where required, pressurization within tolerance of setpoint. Control systems serving spaces requiring high availability must be designed so that component or communication failures do not result in failure of the controlled HVAC equipment. Control and monitoring systems should be powered by a UPS system.

There are a number of ways to accomplish this, but in general the approach is to utilize multiple distributed control systems in a manner such that no system can cause the failure of another system. Where required, HVAC components in the system have dedicated controllers installed to ensure automatic and independent operation of redundant HVAC systems in the event of failures.

Based on Table 2.1, control should be established that provides an inlet condition to data center equipment of 68°F-77°F (20°C-25°C) and telecom equipment of 65°F-80°F (18°C-27°C). Care needs to be taken to ensure that sensors are properly located and tuned. CFD analysis as well as control system simulation may be needed for a successful retrofit.

Where multiple packaged units are provided, regular calibration of controls is also necessary to prevent individual units from working against each other. Errors in control system calibration, differences in unit setpoints, and sensor drift can cause multiple-unit installations to simultaneously heat and cool and/or humidify and dehumidify, wasting a significant amount of energy. Integrated control systems should also be considered that communicate from unit to unit, sharing setpoints and sensor data to ensure teamwork and reduce the potential for units to work against each other. Lead/lag control could also be used if desired. Redundant controllers on packaged units can also be considered to reduce single-point failures.

If chilled water is used, water temperature should be optimized to prevent unnecessary latent cooling.

4.11.2 Monitoring

Datacom facilities often require extensive monitoring of the control and other infrastructure control systems. Multiple interface gateways are often used to ensure that individual system communication interface component failures do not remove access to the total system information database.

Monitoring should include the control system sensors as well as independent "monitoring only" sensors and should include the datacom equipment areas, critical infrastructure equipment rooms, command/network operations centers, etc., to ensure critical parameters are maintained. Sensors should be located at the air inlet of racks and at heights consistent with ASHRAE's *Thermal Guidelines for Data Processing Environments* (ASHRAE 2004h). Monitoring also should be sufficient to ensure anomalies are detected early and with adequate time to allow operating staff time to mitigate and restore conditions prior to equipment impact. Monitored data can facilitate trending, alarming, and troubleshooting efforts.

Examples of parameters worthy of being monitored include underfloor static air pressure, temperature, and humidity, early warning smoke detection systems, ground currents, and rack temperatures and humidity. Monitoring systems can be integral to or separate from the control systems and can be as simple as portable data loggers or strip chart recorders or as complex as high-speed (GPS-synchronized) forensic time stamping of critical breakers and status points. New technologies are becoming available that allow distributed monitoring sensors to be connected to the data and communication network without separate wiring systems.

Because datacom equipment malfunctions may be caused by or attributed to improper control of the datacom equipment room environmental conditions, it may be desirable to keep permanent records of the space temperature and humidity. Many datacom equipment manufacturers already imbed temperature sensors in their equipment, which, in turn, can be correlated with equipment function and also provide for reduced capacity operation or shutdown to avoid equipment damage from overheating.

As a minimum, alarms should be provided to signal when temperature or humidity limits are exceeded. Properly maintained and accurate differential pressure gauges for air-handling equipment filters can help prevent loss of system airflow capacity and maintain design environmental conditions. All monitoring and alarm devices should provide local indication as well as interface to the central monitoring system.

5

Air Distribution

5.1 INTRODUCTION

Air is the main carrier of heat and moisture in a data center facility. As such, air distribution and flow patterns play a major role in determining the temperature and relative humidity in the data center rooms. Delivering the appropriate amount of cold air at the location where heat is generated is a challenging task. Similarly, returning the hot air without mixing with the cold air is also important. Recirculation and excessive mixing of hot return and cold supply airstreams could be detrimental to the performance and life of the servers. Also, short-circuiting of cold air back to air conditioners without passing through the heat-generating servers can significantly affect the performance and the energy efficiency of the air-conditioning units.

Due to a rapid increase in the power and heat densities of servers and other data processing equipment, new technologies involving innovative cooling approaches with liquid are emerging. However, at the time of this writing, telecom offices use no liquid-cooled equipment, and air still remains the most common medium for providing cooling to data center facilities. This chapter describes various methods and associated challenges in effective distribution of cold air from the air-conditioning units to the heat-generating equipment.

5.2 AIRFLOW THROUGH EQUIPMENT

5.2.1 Design Conditions

Air-cooled electronic equipment located in equipment rooms is exposed to the environmental conditions (i.e., temperature and relative humidity) in the aisles from which they draw air. Therefore, the designer of the cooling systems for data spaces must have a design goal for achieving those conditions at the inlets of the equipment. The generally accepted or recommended range of temperature and relative humidity can be found in the references for telecom central offices (Telcordia 2001) and data centers (ASHRAE 2004h).

5.2.2 Once-Through Concept

Once-through cooling means that the cooling air passes through the electronic equipment only once before returning to the air handler. Some recirculation of return air and bypass of supply air are inevitable in almost every real-life arrangement of open style data centers (i.e., equipment rooms in which the cooling air is provided from the aisles and/or adjacent spaces). This is applicable at the room level as well as at the cabinet level. If implemented correctly, however, both the rack cooling and the overall thermal effectiveness can be improved and optimized.

5.2.3 Equipment Cooling Classes

Historically, there was little airflow uniformity among electronic equipment. Some draw cooling air from the front and some from the side. Some exhaust to the rear, some to the side, some to the front, and some out the top. From the package perspective, there were often reasons for this myriad of airflow protocols. However, many of these protocols contributed to a high degree of air mixing in the equipment room and, in turn, poor rack cooling and thermal effectiveness.

Telcordia GR-3028 (Telcordia 2001) introduced Equipment-Cooling (EC) Classes for classifying the location of air intake and air exhaust on electronic equipment. They also developed a universal EC-Class syntax. For example, a piece of equipment with an intake along the front and an exhaust along the rear would be classified as F-R. The classification syntax provides an important "common language." A subset of the syntax has been adopted by the industry (ASHRAE 2004h).

Individual IT equipment (e.g., servers) as well as entire racks of equipment may be classified based on air intake and exhaust locations. Figure 5-1 shows the three recommended airflow protocols: front to rear (F-R), front to top (F-T), and front to top and rear (F-T/R). Cabinet systems and entire racks that follow any of these three protocols will complement a hot-aisle/cold-aisle room configuration. Individual

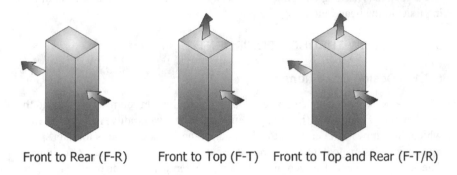

Front to Rear (F-R)   Front to Top (F-T)   Front to Top and Rear (F-T/R)

Figure 5.1 Recommended equipment airflow directivity protocols.

rack-mounted IT equipment should follow the F-R protocol only. Although there are notable exceptions, the trend among equipment manufactures is toward adopting these protocols.

Racks following the recommended protocols draw air directly from the room (only) and therefore do not substantially affect the airflow in the raised-floor air space. However, some preconfigured rack systems and standard rack systems fitted with supplemental cooling products may draw air directly from the raised-floor air space. Special consideration must be given to the use of these products, as they may alter the airflow in the raised-floor air space and potentially reduce the cooling airflow available to other equipment in the data center.

Other products that require special attention include isolated (self-contained) rack systems and systems in which the warm exhaust air is completely ducted back to the facility cooling system.

5.2.4 Blanking Panels

Blanking panels are essential when an equipment shelf or a complete rack is unoccupied in a hot-aisle/cold-aisle configuration. As implied, these panels (e.g., a piece of sheet metal) block air from either recirculating or bypassing through a gap in a rack without passing through equipment. Without the panels, recirculation and bypass generally occur, decreasing rack cooling effectiveness and the thermal effectiveness. Spare blanking panels should be stocked to allow for use as needed when equipment is changed in (or temporarily removed from) a cabinet.

5.2.5 Equipment Airflow

Most equipment incorporates fans, which drive the flow of cool inlet air and hot exhaust air. The airflow rate is largely unaffected by the equipment's environment; however, it may vary based on factors including equipment configuration, inlet temperature, and real-time computing load. The referenced work (ASHRAE 2004h) outlines how equipment manufacturers should report "nominal" and "maximum" airflow along with a typical heat-release rate.

Neighboring IT equipment and racks must utilize similar inlet and exhaust locations in order to promote the separation of cool supply and hot exhaust air. If equipment with different airflow patterns is placed together in the same rack, the hot exhaust air from one piece of equipment may be drawn into the inlet of another piece of equipment.

5.3 AIRFLOW THROUGH EQUIPMENT ROOMS

5.3.1 Hot-Aisle/Cold-Aisle Protocol

The hot-aisle/cold-aisle protocol is a simple and efficient way of promoting the once-through concept at the room level in telecom central offices and data centers (Telcordia 2001; ASHRAE, 2004h). The goal is to create a steady supply of cold air at the front of the racks and extract the hot exhaust air from the rear of the racks. This is best accomplished by aligning racks in rows such that they face front-to-front and rear-to-rear with supply air delivered only to the "cold aisles." The hot-aisle/cold-aisle protocol can be implemented with underfloor, overhead, horizontal displacement, or any other method that dependably supplies the air into cold aisles.

The hot-aisle/cold-aisle protocol does not work well with equipment (or racks) that do not draw air from the front and exhaust to the rear. When the number of such noncomplying racks within an equipment room grows, other cooling protocols must be deployed. Generally, such equipment is best located in a separate area of the equipment room and may require a custom cooling solution.

5.3.2 Placement of Racks

Racks are preferably placed in straight, uniform rows following the hot-aisle/cold-aisle protocol described above. The referenced work (ASHRAE 2004h) includes detailed recommendations for placement of equipment racks, including the aisle pitch, aisle width, etc.

5.3.3 Equipment Room Airflow

To ensure the hot-aisle/cold-aisle protocol, the supply air should be introduced primarily into the cold aisles only. Cable openings located in the hot aisle generally permit some cold air to escape into the hot aisle. And there may be some situations where racks with very high heat loads exhaust very hot air, creating a very uncomfortable servicing area; therefore, some cold air needs to be mixed into this hot region. If applicable, return grilles should be placed so that the hot air can easily migrate back to the air handler without mixing with cold supply air. This generally results in the placement of the returns at a high location within the space.

5.3.4 Cooling Effectiveness

Various methods have been proposed to quantify cooling effectiveness. The following are some examples:

Dimensionless indices to quantify the extent of mixing of return air with supply air (Supply Heat Index, SHI) and also the extent of bypass of supply air to the return airstream (Return Heat Index, RHI) have been proposed (Sharma 2002).

The dimensionless Rack Cooling Index (RCI) is a measure of how effectively equipment racks are cooled within industry thermal guidelines and standards such as ASHRAE and NEBS (Herrlin 2005).

With proper application, these various indices can be used to optimize the design or implementation of a mechanical system or IT layout.

5.4 CFD MODELING

Optimizing cooling performance of a data center is a challenging task. Several factors affect the airflow distribution and the cooling performance of a data center.

Physical measurements and field testing are not only time and labor intensive but sometimes impossible. In such a situation, computational fluid dynamics (CFD) simulations provide a feasible alternative for testing various design layouts and configurations in a relatively short time. CFD simulations can predict the air velocities, pressure, and temperature distribution in the entire data center facility. They can be used, for example, to locate areas of recirculation and short-circuiting or to assess airflow patterns around the racks. In addition, CFD simulations can assist in predicting the nondimensional indices described above for quantifying rack cooling effectiveness and thermal effectiveness. Facilities managers, designers, and consultants can employ these techniques to estimate the performance of a proposed layout before actually building the facility. Likewise, CFD simulations can also provide appropriate insight and guidance in reconfiguring existing facilities toward the same goal of optimizing the facility's cooling system.

For more information on selecting, using, and reporting the results from CFD software, see ASHRAE RP-1133 (ASHRAE 2001a).

5.5 ROOM COOLING CLASSES (PROTOCOLS)

Control of the rack inlet temperatures to the recommended temperature range is the ultimate goal of the room cooling system. The temperature of the cooling air actually available at the equipment inlets depends on the airflow dynamics as the air is delivered from the supply outlet (e.g., perforated floor tile or overhead diffuser) to the equipment inlet. These airflow dynamics vary widely depending on the method of delivery of the air and room layout. Several room-cooling protocols are discussed below.

5.5.1 Syntax for RC-Classes

The referenced work (Telcordia 2001) introduced Room-Cooling (RC) Classes. Each class refers to the way air is distributed and removed from the space. For example, Vertical Underfloor (VUF) Class refers to the traditional data center cooling system with a raised floor and perforated floor tiles; the Vertical Overhead (VOH) Class refers to the traditional telecom central office system with ducted overhead distribution. Telcordia does not establish any preferred classes.

5.5.2 Vertical Underfloor (VUF)

VUF refers to the delivery of air from an underfloor space, i.e., a raised-floor air space. This is, by far, the most common type of air delivery method for data centers. In a typical VUF system, AHU or CRAC units supply conditioned air into the raised-floor air space; the air exits this air space through perforated floor tiles located near the inlets of electronic equipment racks.

Electronic equipment will draw air as needed and, if sufficient cooling air is unavailable, warm exhaust air will be consumed, i.e., recirculated, from over the racks or around the row ends. Being a "bottom-up" displacement type system, a good starting point is to supply slightly more air than the total airflow drawn into the equipment.

To achieve predictable performance, most VUF data centers are designed to deliver the same airflow rate through each perforated tile. If only one type of perforated tile is deployed, the airflow will be uniform provided the raised-floor air space is uniformly pressurized. Raised-floor air space pressure uniformity is affected by a number of factors, including placement of electronic equipment, perforated floor tiles, and AHU/CRAC units; the location and nature of leakage paths; raised-floor air space depth; perforated tile type; and the size and location of airflow obstructions in the raised-floor air space. As stated earlier, temperatures within a specified range at the rack inlets is the ultimate goal; however, where new construction is planned and a rack layout is not yet developed, CFD modeling can be a valuable design tool for use in determining the pressure distribution (and, therefore, perforated tile flow rates) in the raised-floor air space. As such, designing for a uniform pressure distribution is a good starting point for designing a data center with predictable performance. Similarly, it may be necessary to verify the as-built design through measurement.

Factors affecting the air delivery and overall performance of a VUF system are discussed below; see references VanGilder (2005) and Schmidt (2001b) for more information.

1. **Placement of Electronic Equipment and Floor Tiles:** A good starting point for many installations is the standard 7-tile-pitch hot-aisle/cold-aisle layout as discussed in and shown in Figure 5-2 (ASHRAE 2004h). Rooms should be rectangular as much as possible with regular, symmetric, or repeating layouts. Only F-R, F-T, or F-T/R class equipment should be used with the hot-aisle/cold-aisle architecture.

2. **Placement of AHU/CRAC Units:** AHU/CRAC units are often placed around the perimeter of the room as shown in Figure 5-2. With this layout, units should generally be located at the ends of the hot aisles in order to maximize the distance between the high-velocity supply airflow and the perforated tiles and to provide an efficient path for warm return air in the room. Turning vanes—used to turn the AHU/CRAC unit air supply stream(s) from a downward to a horizontal flow direction—are generally unnecessary. In fact, perforated tile airflow uniformity may be improved by simply allowing the supply airstream to diffuse quickly and evenly after impinging directly upon the subfloor. Again, CFD modeling is a valuable design tool for optimizing a specific layout.

3. **Leakage Airflow:** Cable and utility cutouts and gaps around tiles and other openings in the raised floor, which are not intended for supplying cool air, result in "leakage airflow." Anecdotal evidence indicates that leakage airflow can amount to anywhere from 10% to 50% or more of the total airflow supplied to the raised-floor air space. High leakage rates result in poor uniformity of airflow through the perforated tiles and poor cooling efficiency due to the loss

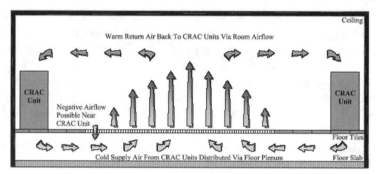

Sectional View (A-A)

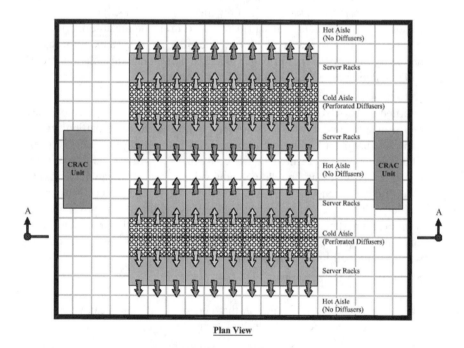

Plan View

Figure 5.2 Schematic of a datacom equipment room with underfloor raised-floor air space supply air distribution.

in control of separation of the cool supply and warm return airflow. Minimizing the size of tile cutouts and using products designed to seal unavoidable openings will reduce leakage airflow.

4. **Raised-Floor Air Space Depth and Obstructions:** Raised-floor air space is commonly used for both air distribution and data/power cabling and piping. Underfloor cabling can substantially disrupt the distribution of supply air in the raised-floor air space. Further, the effects of obstructions are often localized, creating uneven cooling performance around the data center. Raised-floor air space depth should generally be designed for a minimum of 24 inches of clear space. Greater raised-floor air space depth can help achieve a more uniform pressure distribution in some cases. Each data center should have a cable management strategy to minimize airflow obstructions caused by power and communications cables, wires, etc.

5. **Perforated Tile Type:** Nominally 25%-open perforated tiles should generally be used, as they provide a good balance of low pressure drop and relatively uniform underfloor pressure. High flow tiles (e.g., 56% open) can allow more airflow at a given pressure but lead to less uniform and predictable distributions. It is possible to mix low and high flow tiles in a single system, but it may be necessary to verify the performance of such a nonstandard installation through CFD modeling or through testing and measurement.

6. **Return Air Paths:** In a VUF system, hot equipment exhaust air may be returned to the AHU/CRAC units "through the room" or through an overhead return air space or ductwork, as shown in Figure 5-2. However, particular attention must be given to this "return migration" path during the design process. This involves leaving sufficient space between the tops of the racks and the ceiling (or roof) such that the relatively low velocity return air can get across the room and back to the AHU/CRAC unit inlets. Often, return duct extensions are built over the CRAC units in order to effectively facilitate the removal of hot air from the highest points in the space. AHUs, being typically larger than CRAC units, may require partial-height walls around the units to encourage only the warmer return air to enter the unit inlets.

7. **Strengths of VUF systems:**

   a. A VUF system is flexible in that cool air distribution can be modified through placement and relocation of perforated tiles.

   b. VUF, being the most common for conventional data centers, is the most familiar to building engineers and IT managers.

   c. VUF delivery is generally compatible with a fault-tolerant, i.e., redundant, mechanical design.

   d. The raised-floor air space can provide a convenient space through which other infrastructure, such as piping, cabling, etc., can be routed.

8. **Issues of concern for VUF systems:**

    a. Unless the entire facility is placed on a raised floor, including ancillary spaces, some of the data space raised-floor area may be lost to ramps.

    b. It can be difficult to keep the raised-floor air space clean, organized, and free of obstructions for optimized airflow.

    c. The ability to route portions of the mechanical, electrical, or networking infrastructure through the raised-floor space is listed in the previous section as a "strength." The same can be interpreted as an issue of concern — if the raised floor is to be used for the installation of any of this infrastructure, care must be taken to provide sufficient extra height to the raised floor to optimize the airflow distribution throughout the raised-floor air space.

    d. It may be difficult to achieve uniform raised-floor air space pressurization and, consequently, predictable or desired airflow through perforated tiles.

    e. Security may be a concern. Undesirable or dangerous materials can be stored in the raised-floor air space, and the raised-floor air space may provide uncontrolled access to cabling, infrastructure, or other secure parts of the facility.

    f. A VUF system operating with insufficient airflow (relative to equipment needs) may exhibit a sharp discontinuity in air temperatures within the cold aisle due to the recirculation of warm air over or around the racks at the ends of the rows. Equipment located just below a critical height may receive cooling air very close to the temperature of the raised-floor air space, while equipment located just above this critical height may receive air that is substantially warmer.

5.5.3 Overhead (VOH)

VOH refers to the delivery of air from overhead ductwork. Air is conditioned by built-up AHUs or CRAC units and is supplied near the electronic equipment inlets via diffusers. Multiple AHUs or CRAC units may serve a single manifold or trunk duct as required for redundancy. Warm air extracts are typically located at the high points of the data enter. The VOH system is the most common type of air delivery method for telecom central offices.

As with VUF data centers, airflow dynamics in the room determine actual equipment inlet temperatures. Being a "top down" type of mixing system, a good starting point is to supply slightly less air than the total airflow drawn into the equipment. Unlike a VUF system in which cooling air "displaces" surrounding warm air, a VOH system is typically designed for some intentional mixing of cooling air with the surrounding room air before it is supplied to the equipment.

Factors affecting the performance of this type of air delivery system are addressed below:

1. **Placement of Electronic Equipment**: As with a VUF system, a VOH system should also be organized into hot-aisle/cold-aisle layouts using only F-R or F-T class equipment as much as possible. Rooms should be rectangular and regular in shape, to the extent possible; row spacing should be similar to that used with the VUF system.

2. **Placement of Ductwork and Diffusers:** By necessity, data center ductwork will be large. Typically, branch ducts are aligned over the cold aisles, and diffusers are selected to deliver air in a downward direction into the cold aisles, as shown in Figure 5-3. A balance is often sought in optimizing between low velocity/low pressure drop while maintaining as low a number of diffusers as possible.

3. **Overhead Obstructions:** The area between the supply diffusers and equipment inlets (i.e., the cold aisle) must be kept free of obstructions. This may be more of a challenge with a VOH, which often does not include a raised floor. In this case, all overhead cables and utility lines should be placed above the cabinets or hot aisles.

4. **Return Air Paths:** Particular attention must be given to the path of return air. Leave sufficient space between the tops of the racks and the ceiling (or roof) to create a low-velocity area through which warm air can return unimpeded to the AHUs or CRAC units. Although return locations should generally be as high in the space as practical, upflow AHUs and CRAC units have return air inlets near the floor. Therefore, it may be necessary to duct the returns or create partial-height walls around the units to encourage only the warm return air to be captured at the unit inlets. To facilitate an undisturbed return air path, the supply air diffusers should be dropped to a level below the return air path.

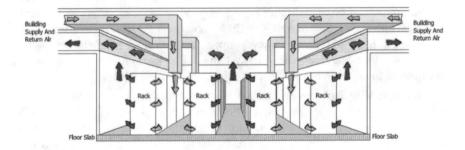

Figure 5.3 Typical ducted ceiling distribution used in datacom facilities.

5. **Strengths of a VOH system:**

   a. The ductwork of a VOH system may be balanced in a straightforward and predictable manner. This enables a system to be tailored to deliver air only where it is needed. (*Note*: the VUF system can also be adjusted through relocation of perforated tiles, but this level of control is not as refined as what is achievable through ducted systems.)

   b. Large AHUs (which, in general, are more easily applied when the air-side system feeds into a large ductwork system) can be more energy efficient than similarly sized systems using CRAC units and underfloor air distribution. With built-up AHUs, more opportunity exists for implementing air-side economizers.

   c. VOH systems can be effective at delivering good temperature distributions at rack inlets. Some studies have indicated that under certain room configurations and design conditions, VOH systems can achieve more uniform inlet conditions at the racks when compared to VUF systems (Herrlin 2005; Sorell 2005). The reason for this may relate to the entrainment and mixing in the aisle that the supply airflow induces when it is delivered from overhead ductwork. Although this may seem contrary to the goals of separating hot and cold airstreams, the tempering or mixing of the higher-velocity air in the cold aisle ensures a more uniform temperature distribution across the fronts of the racks and a lesser sensitivity to drift from the design point.

   d. With a mixing type system, there is an opportunity to provide less supply air than would be provided for a corresponding VUF system, as the discharge temperature off the cooling coil can be set below the recommended supply air condition of the racks with the knowledge that mixing will temper this supply air prior to entry to the datacom equipment.

6. **Issues of concern for VOH systems:**

   a. For systems utilizing large ductwork, the ductwork itself may interfere with some of the return air paths. This issue needs to be fully addressed during the design process to ensure that there is sufficient free area throughout the space to allow for effective return.

   b. Although ductwork systems can be precisely balanced to account for relocation of loads within a space, the balancing procedure can be more complex than the simple relocation or placement of tiles such as in VUF systems.

   c. Air velocities in the cold aisles in VOH systems are usually higher than normally found in VUF systems. This may lead to comfort-related complaints from those working in the space.

   d. Care must be made in using CRAC units as part of ducted systems, since the external static pressure of these units is typically much more limited than for central air-handling systems.

5.5.4 Horizontal Displacement (HDP)

HDP air distribution systems are used predominantly in telecommunications central offices in Europe and Asia. Typically, this system introduces air horizontally from one end of a cold aisle. A large volume of slightly cooled air moves along the aisle at low velocity. Subsequently, the electronic equipment draws necessary cold air from the cold aisle. This system does require that a significant amount of floor space be reserved for the large diffusers, which are required to make the displacement approach work. Additionally, the length of the equipment aisles and the equipment heat density are limiting factors.

5.5.5 Horizontal Overhead (HOH)

HOH air distribution system is used by some long-distance carriers in North America. This system introduces the supply air horizontally above the cold aisles and is generally utilized in raised-floor environments where the raised floor is used for cabling.

5.5.6 Natural Convection Overhead (NOH)

NOH air distribution cooling strategy is not commonly used. In this approach, cooling coils are suspended from the ceiling. Since the cooling "units" cool the rising hot air due to buoyancy, there are no fans or ducts in this room design.

5.5.7 Supplemental Cooling

Upgrading an entire equipment room to a higher heat load density is a complicated and expensive process. Supplemental cooling, however, can be introduced with reasonable effort to solve the cooling issues in localized hot areas and to promote once-through cooling.

Chapter four of *Datacom Equipment Power Trends and Applications* (ASHRAE 2005i) describes various methods of providing local or supplemental cooling, which are as follows:

a. Fan systems that pull air directly from the underfloor raised-floor air space and deliver it to the front of the IT equipment within the rack.
b. Fan systems that take hot exhaust air directly from the rack and return it to the computer room's air handlers.
c. Closed-loop cooling enclosures, typically using chilled water, which condition the air within the enclosure to maintain a locally controlled environment.
d. Overhead coolers located over the rack and/or at the center of the cold aisles receive hot air from the hot aisle and supply the cold air into the cold aisle. This method facilitates the delivery of cold air from the top and the return of the hot exhaust air from the hot aisles locally to the overhead chillers.
e. Rack rear door coolers, which cool the hot equipment exhaust air.

6

Liquid Cooling

As discussed in the previous chapter, the heat load in server racks may be exceeding air cooling limits both at the microprocessor level and within a data center, thereby driving designs to employ liquid-cooled solutions. Data centers might also be employing liquid cooling to reduce overall cost associated with the cooling of the data center equipment. As a recap, for the purposes of this book, the definitions of air and liquid cooling are:

a. **Air Cooling**—Conditioned air is supplied to the inlets of the rack/cabinet/server for convection cooling of the heat rejected by the components of the electronic equipment within the rack. It is understood that within the rack, the transport of heat from the actual source component (e.g., CPU) within the rack itself can be either liquid or air based, but the heat rejection media from the rack to the building's cooling device outside the rack is air. The use of heat pipes or pumped loops inside a server or rack where the liquid remains is still considered air cooling.

b. **Liquid Cooling**—Conditioned liquid is supplied to the inlets of the rack/cabinet/server for thermal cooling of the heat rejected by the components of the electronic equipment within the rack. It is understood that within the rack, the transport of heat from the actual source component (e.g., CPU) within the rack itself can be either liquid or air based (or any other heat transfer mechanism), but the heat rejection media to the building cooling device outside the rack is liquid.

The scope of this chapter is limited to the heat rejection associated with rack/cabinet cooling and does not include the intricacies of component or board level cooling at a component level. There are various liquid cooling methods (e.g., heat pipes, thermosyphons, etc.) used to transport heat from the source component (e.g., CPU) to a location elsewhere, either within the packaging of the electronic equipment or another location within the rack/cabinet itself, but this level of cooling is not discussed in this chapter.

For the purposes of this chapter, we will define the liquid used to transport the heat from the electronic equipment to another location outside the rack as being the "transport liquid." The liquid cooling methods considered all require a means of rejecting heat from the transport liquid to the larger building cooling system.

6.1   LIQUID COOLING OVERVIEW

As heat load densities continue to rise, so does the challenge of cooling with air due to the limits of heat sink/air moving device performance and rack level acoustic limitations. Liquids, primarily because of their higher density, are much more effective in the removal of heat than air, making liquid cooling a more viable choice as the concentration of thermal loads becomes more dense.

Within liquid cooling systems, piping connects the liquid cooling media directly to the electronic equipment components. The attributes described below provide some insight into the significant thermal performance advantages that are possible by using a fluid rather than air as the source of cooling:

- The volumetric heat-carrying capacity of water is 3500 times greater than air at sea level conditions and at atmospheric pressure.
- The volumetric heat-carrying capacity of a refrigerant that changes state to a gas as it absorbs heat is five to seven times the capacity of water when both are in a liquid state.
- The heat transfer capability of water is 2 to 3 orders of magnitude greater than air.

Although liquid cooling systems were prevalent as a means for cooling mainframe computer systems, they fell out of favor with the advent of semiconductor technologies that did not initially require it but now are approaching limits that may again require some form of liquid cooling.

6.2   DATACOM FACILITY CHILLED-WATER SYSTEMS

Chilled water may be provided by either a small chiller matched in capacity to the computer equipment or a branch of the chilled-water system serving the air-handling units. Design and installation of chilled water or refrigerant piping and selection of the operating temperatures should minimize the potential for leaks and condensation, especially in the computer room, while satisfying the requirements of the systems served.

Chilled-water systems for liquid-cooled computer equipment must be designed to:

1. provide water at a temperature and pressure as specified within the manufacturer's tolerances and
2. be capable of operating year-round, 24 hours per day.

Chilled-water distribution systems should be designed to the same standards of quality, reliability, and flexibility as other computer room support systems. Where growth is likely, the chilled-water system should be designed for expansion or addition of new equipment without a required shutdown of the existing computer room equipment.

Figure 4-2 illustrates a looped chilled-water system with sectional valves and multiple valved branch connections. The branches could serve air handlers or water-cooled computer equipment. The valves permit modifications or repairs without complete shutdown.

Chilled-water piping must be pressure tested, fully insulated, and protected with an effective vapor retarder. The test pressure should be applied in increments to all sections of pipe in the computer area. Drip pans piped to an effective drain should be placed below any valves or other components in the computer room that cannot be satisfactorily insulated, and water lines should be sleeved with waterproof coverings that will drain any leaks or condensation to drip pans. A strainer should be installed in the inlet to local cooling equipment to prevent control valve and heat exchanger passages from clogging.

If cross-connections with other systems are made, possible effects on the computer room system of the introduction of dirt, scale, or other impurities must be addressed.

6.3   LIQUID-COOLED COMPUTER EQUIPMENT

The most common approach for cooling computers today is with forced air cooling. However, with the increased microprocessor power densities and rack heat loads, some equipment will require liquid cooling to maintain the equipment within the environmental specifications required by the manufacturer.

Manufacturers would normally supply the cooling system as part of the computer equipment and the liquid loop would be internal to the equipment. However, the transfer of heat from the liquid-cooled computer system to the environment housing the racks takes place through a liquid-to-liquid heat exchanger.

Figure 6-1 shows a liquid loop internal to the rack where the exchange of heat with the room occurs with a liquid-to-air heat exchanger. In this case, the rack appears as an air-cooled rack to the client and is classified as an air-cooled system. It is included here to show the evolution to liquid-cooled systems. Figure 6-2 depicts a similar liquid loop internal to the rack used to cool the electronics within the rack, but in this case the heat exchange is with a liquid-to-liquid heat exchanger. Typically the liquid circulating within the rack is maintained above dew point to eliminate any condensation concerns. Figure 6-3 depicts a design very similar to Figure 6-2 but where some of the primary liquid loop components are housed outside the rack to permit more space within the rack for electronic components.

A further extension of these designs are hybrid systems where both liquid and air cooling exist within the rack. These are shown in Figures 6-4, 6-5, and 6-6. These

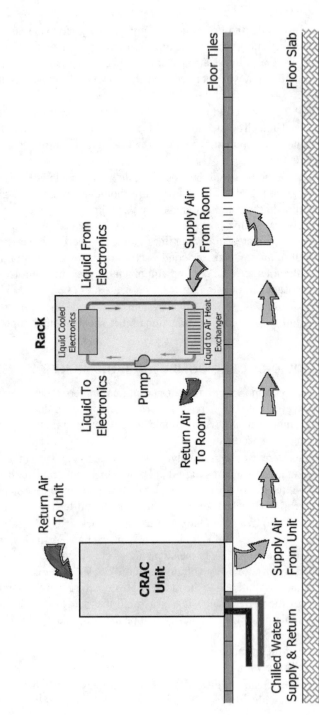

Figure 6.1 Internal liquid cooling loop restricted to within rack extents.

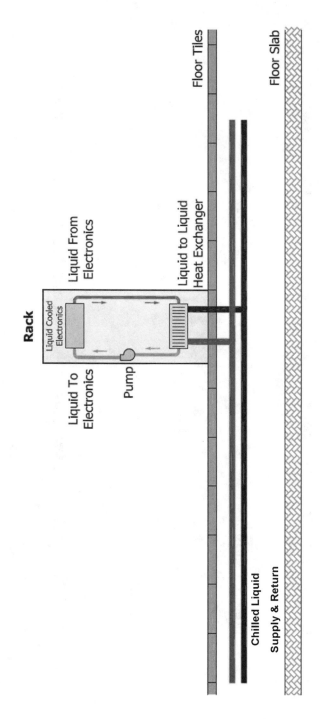

Figure 6.2 Internal liquid cooling loop within rack extents and external liquid cooling loop to racks.

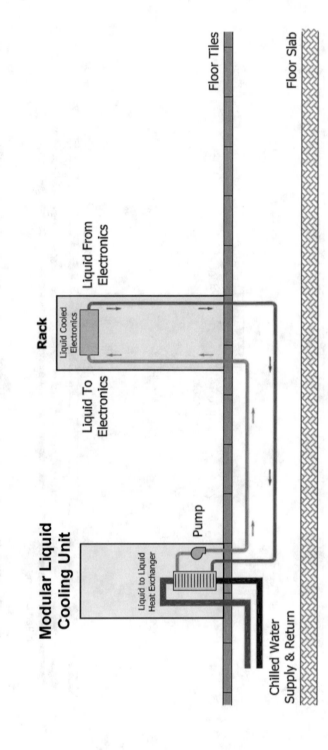

Figure 6.3 Internal liquid cooling loop extended to liquid-cooled external modular cooling unit.

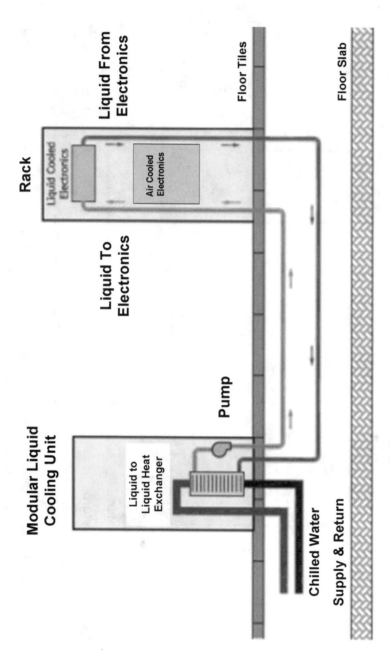

Figure 6.4 Hybrid rack cooling system—internal liquid cooling loop extended to liquid-cooled external modular cooling unit and rack air-cooled components.

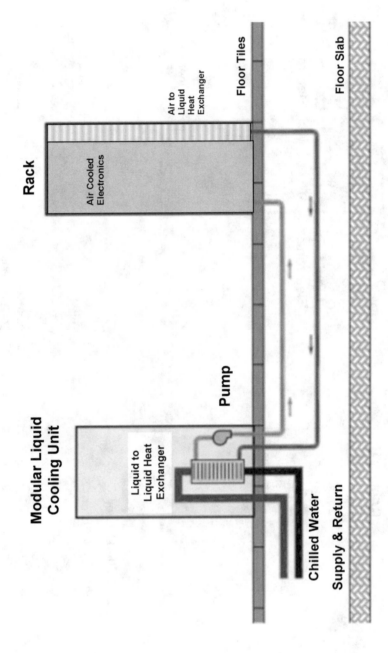

Figure 6.5 Hybrid rack cooling system—rack level liquid cooling loop extended to liquid-cooled external modular cooling unit and rack air-cooled components.

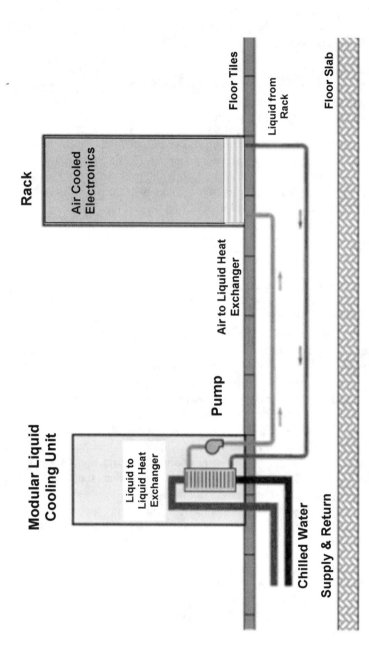

Figure 6.6 Hybrid rack cooling system—rack level liquid cooling loop extended to liquid-cooled external modular cooling unit and rack air-cooled components.

would be more typical of electronic systems employing liquid since some air cooling generally always exists within the rack.

The liquid loops for cooling the electronics shown in Figures 6-1 through 6-6 are typically of three types:

- Dielectric fluids
- Water (or water/glycol mix but referred to as simply "water" throughout this section for clarity)
- Refrigerants (pumped and vapor compression)

Observe that the name for each type of cooling method actually refers to the coolant that is used to cool the computer equipment. Each option requires a path (pipes or hoses) for the coolant to flow, and work (pump or compressor) to force the coolant through the system. Each option includes some combination of valves, sensors, heat exchanger, and control logic within the cooling circuit.

Once the priorities of the system design have been established, the "best" cooling option is selected. Some of the relative merits/trade-offs for the three primary methodologies follow.

6.4   COOLING LIQUIDS

6.4.1   Dielectric Fluids

Dielectric fluids exhibit properties that make an attractive heat transfer media for data processing applications. Foremost is an ability to contact the electronics directly (eliminating some of the intermediary heat exchange steps), as well as the transfer of high heat loads (via an evaporative cooling methodology). This technology has containment concerns, metallurgical compatibility exposures, and tight operating tolerances. Dielectric liquids are not to be confused with chlorinated fluorocarbons (CFCs), which are subject to environmental concerns.

The heat that is rejected by the dielectric liquids is either rejected through a liquid-to-air heat exchanger (Figure 6-1) or to a dielectric liquid-to-water heat exchanger (Figures 6-2 through 6-6) where the central plant supplies the chilled water to remove the heat. Liquid transfer, for high-density heat loads and where the system heat loads are high, is the optimum design point for product design and client requirements. There are several reasons for choosing a dielectric liquid cooling strategy:

- Less conversion losses (fewer steps between the heat load and the ultimate heat sink). The heat transfer path could be from the electronic circuit to dielectric liquid to central plant chilled water.
- Heat transfer capacity of dielectric liquids is several orders of magnitude higher compared to air.
- Minimal acoustical concerns.
- More compact.

6.4.2   Water

The new ASHRAE thermal guidelines (ASHRAE 2004h) state that the maximum dew point for a class 1 environment is 63°F (17°C). With this requirement the logical design point would be to provide water to the electronics above 63°F (17°C) to eliminate any condensation concerns.

The heat that is rejected by this water is either rejected through a water-to-air heat exchanger (Figure 6-1) or to a water-to-water heat exchanger (Figures 6-2 through 6-6) where the central plant supplies the chilled water to remove the heat. Liquid transfer, for high-density heat loads and where the system heat loads are high, is the optimum design point for product design and client requirements. There are several reasons for choosing a water cooling strategy:

- Less conversion losses (fewer steps between the heat load and the ultimate heat sink). The heat transfer path would be from the electronic circuit to component interface, to water, to central plant chilled water.
- Heat transfer capacity of water compared to dielectric liquids and air (water has several times and several orders of magnitude higher specific heat capacity compared to dielectric liquid and air, respectively.
- Minimal acoustical concerns.
- More compact than air or dielectric liquid cooling.

6.4.3   Refrigerants

Refrigerants can be used either in a pumped loop technique or vapor compression cycle. The advantages of using refrigerants are similar to those of dielectric liquids in that they can contact the electronics without shorting out any of the electronics.

In most cases, the refrigerant requires the liquid lines to use copper piping or corrugated hoses instead of rubber hose to limit the loss of refrigerant over time. In the pumped loop methodology, the refrigerant is at a low pressure such that, when passing through an evaporator, the liquid evaporates or passes into a two-phase flow situation and then passes onto the condenser where the cycle begins again. If lower than ambient temperatures are desired, then a vapor compression cycle may be employed.

Clients view a system employing refrigerant as a "dry" liquid such that any leak that does occur does not damage any of the electronics nor does it cause the electronics to fail when in operating mode. This may thus be viewed by some clients as the preferred or even required cooling methodology over "wet" liquid cooling technologies such as water. Environmental considerations of refrigerant-based cooling methods should be taken into consideration, as well as the possibility of interference with fire suppression systems.

6.5   RELIABILITY

System reliability is so vital that the potential cost of system failure may justify redundant systems, capacity, and/or components. The designer should identify potential points of failure that could cause the system to interrupt critical data processing applications and should provide redundant or backup systems.

It may be desirable to cross-connect chilled-water or refrigeration equipment for backup, as suggested for air-handling equipment. A strategy for configuring the piping system and components must be planned to achieve the desired level of reliability or availability. This applies not only to chilled-water systems but to any liquid cooling system. Redundant refrigeration may be required, the extent of the redundancy depending on the importance of the computer installation. In many cases, standby power for the computer room air-conditioning system is justified.

Cooling systems are as critical as electrical systems and therefore must be planned to continuously perform during a power outage. Especially in high-density situations, the equipment temperatures can very quickly exceed their operational limits during the time that the generators are being started, the power being transferred, and the cooling system being restarted.

To achieve the desired continuous operation during a power outage can require certain cooling equipment to be supplied from an uninterruptible power supply (UPS) while other equipment waits for the emergency generators to be fully operational. Another measure may involve the use of a liquid standby storage. In the case of chilled water, this can be achieved through the use of thermal storage tanks that could provide sufficient cooling until the full cooling system is restored to full operation. Where cooling towers or other configurations that require makeup water are used, sufficient water storage on the premises should be considered. This provision is to protect against a loss of water service to the site.

Typical storage strategies for makeup water are similar to generator fuel storage (e.g., 24, 48, 72 hours of reserve or more) and can result in the need for very large, multiple storage tanks, depending on the scale of the installation, so the impact to the site is a significant one and may be problematic if not planned.

As previously mentioned, there is often a concern over the presence of liquids near electronic equipment. Liquid cooling, however, was effectively used for many years in the mainframe environment. Just as with any other design condition or parameter, liquid cooling requires effective planning, but it can be accomplished and the desired level of reliability achieved.

See chapter 13 for more information about availability and reliability.

Part II

Other Considerations

7

Ancillary Spaces

Space must be allocated within a datacom facility for storage of components and material, support equipment, operations, and servicing of the datacom equipment. Some ancillary spaces may require environmental conditions comparable to those of the datacom equipment, while others may have less stringent requirements. Component and material storage areas often require environmental conditions comparable to those of the datacom equipment. Support equipment areas often have less stringent environmental requirements, but their continuous operation is often vital to the proper functioning of the datacom facility.

7.1 ELECTRICAL POWER DISTRIBUTION EQUIPMENT

Electrical power distribution equipment can typically tolerate more variation and a wider range of temperature and humidity than datacom equipment. Equipment in this category includes incoming service/distribution switchgear, switchboard, automatic transfer switches, panelboards, and transformers. Figure 7.1 provides a block diagram of the typical configuration of electrical power distribution equipment in a datacom facility. Manufacturers' data should be checked to determine the amount of heat release and design conditions for satisfactory operation. Building, electrical, and fire codes should be checked to identify when equipment must be enclosed to prevent unauthorized access or housed in a separate room.

Uninterruptible Power Supplies (UPSs): Uninterruptible power supplies come in a variety of configurations but most often use batteries as the energy storage medium. They are usually configured to provide redundancy for the central power buses and typically operate continuously at less than full-load capacity. UPSs must be air conditioned with sufficient redundancy and diversity to provide an operable system throughout an emergency or accident. The relationship between load and heat release is usually nonlinear. Verification with the equipment vendor is necessary to properly size the HVAC system.

UPS power monitoring and conditioning (rectifier and inverter) equipment is usually the primary source of heat release. This equipment usually has self-

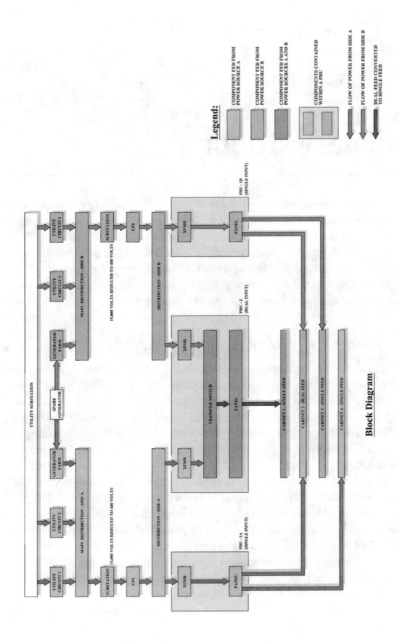

Figure 7.1 Typical electrical power distribution equipment block diagram.

contained cooling fans that draw intake air from the floor level or the face of the equipment and discharge the heated air at the top of the equipment. The design of the air distribution system should take into account the position of the UPS equipment air intakes and discharges. Heat release is related to efficiency, and the cooling load can be minimized by selecting UPS equipment that is efficient both at part-load and full-load conditions.

7.2   BATTERY PLANTS

7.2.1   Secondary Battery Plants

The installation of secondary battery plants that serve as a temporary backup power source should generally be in accordance with NFPA 70, Article 480, "Storage Batteries" (NFPA 2002d). It is also good practice to check with the local building department and fire department officials for any local installation requirements. Other relevant sources of guidance are NFPA 70E, *Standard for Electrical Safety in the Workplace* (NFPA 2004), and NFPA 76, *Recommended Practice for the Fire Protection of Telecommunications Facilities* (NFPA 2002f).

The remainder of this section on secondary battery plants is intended to pertain to typical installations utilized in datacom facilities where the battery plant voltage is 24 or 48 VDC and plant storage capacity is well in excess of 10 ampere-hours at the 1-hour rate.

Battery plants are typically required by code to be enclosed to prevent unauthorized access. These plants often have exposed electrical conductors, connectors, and terminals, and the batteries themselves contain hazardous chemicals. The necessary enclosure may consist of a battery cabinet, a cage, enclosing partitions or walls, or a vault. It is not intended that battery plants must be isolated from any other equipment. In datacom facilities it is common for the battery plant to be located outside the datacom equipment room. With increasing criticality of the datacom facility, it is common for the battery plant to be correspondingly isolated from other equipment.

Battery plants should be provided with a temperature-controlled environment. A temperature of "77°F (25°C) in North America and 68°F (20°C)" in other parts of the world are standard for the rating of batteries for both discharge capacity and life expectancy (IEEE 2005). This tends to lead to batteries with designs optimized for operation at these temperatures. Batteries operated at lower temperatures have lower discharge capacities and longer life expectancies. For batteries operated at higher temperatures, the opposite is the case. It is common for the battery plant to be sized at standard temperature.

During normal operation, the batteries are merely being held at float voltage, and heat gain to the space from the batteries is negligible. During off-normal events of discharging, recharging or equalizing the heat gain to the space from the batteries is still minimal.

For purposes of cooling load calculations, it is common not to include any heat release for the batteries.

When a battery plant is located in the same space as other heat-producing equipment, the cooling system for the other equipment can typically be arranged to provide an adequate temperature-controlled environment for the battery plant.

When the battery plant is isolated from all other heat-producing equipment, some means of heating and cooling the batteries must be established. This can consist of any of the following:

- A dedicated cooling unit sized for envelope and lighting loads.
- A small variable-air-volume branch off a central cooling system.
- Mechanically induced transfer of room air from an adjacent space.

During an abnormal event, such as a malfunctioning battery charger overcharging the batteries, substantial thermal energy can be released from the batteries. In this situation the energy potential is limited by the capacity of the battery charger. This energy is expended on the electrolysis of water molecules in the battery electrolyte into gaseous hydrogen and oxygen and other chemical reactions within the battery. The remainder is converted into thermal energy. The apportionment is beyond the scope of this document.

The actual temperature setpoint should take into account the method used to enclose the batteries. The designer of the power plant should also be consulted prior to establishment of a temperature setpoint.

When a battery plant is physically isolated, it is considered good practice to provide the area with alarms that sound at a continuously monitored location on high temperature or low temperature.

"Hydrogen molecules are small and light, which means that they disperse easily and can be prevented from accumulating with a minimum amount of air movement" (IEEE 2005). According to NFPA codes, however, battery plants must be ventilated to remove heat and any liberated hydrogen gas. Principally, the design of the ventilation system is dictated by the type of batteries, where they are located, and how they are enclosed.

7.2.2 Vented Lead-Acid (VLA) batteries

In addition to the previously listed standards, the installation of VLA batteries must typically be in accordance with IEEE Standard 484, *Recommended Practice for Installation Design and Installation of Vented Lead-Acid Storage Batteries for Stationary Applications* (IEEE 2002a) and the following:

When VLA batteries are isolated in a separate room, whether enclosed in battery cabinets or open to the room, the room must typically be constructed in accordance with the requirements for a "Battery Room."

When VLA batteries represent a minor occupancy of an overall space that is continuously ventilated, and it has been judged that the air circulation and ventilation in the overall space is adequate to limit hydrogen concentration in the overall space from exceeding 1% due to liberated hydrogen from the batteries, then no special battery ventilation system is necessary. Some methods for judging whether an overall space is adequately ventilated are as follows:

- Overall space ventilation system has:

Continuous Minimum Outside Air (cfm) > 1 (cfm/ft^2) × *Battery Plant Footprint* (ft^2) × 2

- Central ventilation system has, for each space it serves housing a battery plant, continuous supply air from central system of:

Supply Air to Room (cfm) > 1 (cfm/ft^2) × *Total Battery Plant Footprint* (ft^2) × 2 × *Total Ventilation System Airflow/Continuous Minimum Outside Airflow*

When an area has been judged as adequately ventilated, an effort should be made to position ventilation system return or relief air openings such that excess return air or relief air is drawn from the battery plant area to create a general movement of room air from the remainder of the open area toward the battery plant. This is intended to control the spread of fumes, gases, or electrolyte spray into other parts of the space.

7.2.3   Valve Regulated Lead-Acid (VRLA) Batteries

VRLA batteries come in a number of different forms such as "absorbed electrolyte," "gelled electrolyte," and others.

In addition to the previously listed standards, the installation of VRLA batteries must typically be in accordance with IEEE Standard 1187, *IEEE Recommended Practice for Installation Design and Installation of Valve-Regulated Lead-Acid Storage Batteries for Stationary Applications* (IEEE 2002b) and the following.

When VRLA type batteries are isolated in a separate room, whether enclosed in battery cabinets or open to the room, the room must typically be constructed in accordance with the requirements for a "Battery Room."

When VRLA batteries represent a minor occupancy of an overall space that is continuously ventilated, and it has been judged that the air circulation and ventilation in the overall space is adequate to limit hydrogen concentration in the overall space from exceeding 1% due to liberated hydrogen from the batteries, then no special battery ventilation system is necessary. Some methods for judging whether an overall space is adequately ventilated are as follows:

- Overall space ventilation system has:

Continuous Minimum Outside Air (cfm) > 1 (cfm/ft^2) × *Battery Plant Footprint* (ft^2) × 2

- Central ventilation system has, for each space it serves housing a battery plant, continuous supply air from central system of:

Supply Air to Room (cfm) > 1 (cfm/ft^2) × *Total Battery Plant Footprint* (ft^2) × 2 × *Total Ventilation System Airflow/Continuous Minimum Outside Airflow*

When an area has been judged as adequately ventilated, an effort should be made to position ventilation system return or relief air openings such that excess return air or relief air is drawn from the battery plant area to create a general movement of room air from the remainder of the open area toward the battery plant. This is intended to control the spread of fumes or gases into other parts of the space.

7.2.4 Battery Rooms

NFPA 70E, *Standard for Electrical Safety in the Workplace* (NFPA 2004), and NFPA 76, *Recommended Practice for the Fire Protection of Telecommunications Facilities* (NFPA 2002f), provide excellent guidance on the construction of battery rooms.

According to the NFPA codes, battery rooms must have ventilation systems to remove any liberated hydrogen. The ventilation systems commonly utilize a forced exhaust with 1 cfm/ft^2 capacity and run continuously unless hydrogen detectors are incorporated to start the ventilation system upon detection of hydrogen.

NFPA codes require that battery rooms be maintained at a negative pressure to adjacent rooms and exhausted to the outside to prevent the migration of fumes, gases or electrolytic spray to other areas.

It is common for makeup air to be drawn for an adjacent area. This may eliminate the need for a separate HVAC system for the battery room, if temperatures are compatible.

With increasing criticality of the datacom facility, it is common that more intensive techniques be employed to mitigate the hazard associated with hydrogen gas buildup. Some examples are:

Redundant ventilation/exhaust systems
Fan failure alarms
Hydrogen detectors to activate backup ventilation systems or send alarms
Explosion-proof equipment (fan motors, switches)
Ventilation fans with nonsparking fan wheels
Controls to regularly exercise the ventilation system

7.3 ENGINE/GENERATOR ROOMS

Engine-driven generators used for primary or emergency power require large amounts of ventilation when running. This equipment is easier to start if a low ambient temperature is avoided. Low-temperature start problems are often reduced in cold climates through use of engine block heaters. Block heater control should be carefully designed to minimize energy use and overheating. Design considerations should also ensure that exhaust air does not recirculate back to any building ventilation air intakes.

Spring-return motorized dampers are typically provided on the air inlets and discharges and maintained normally closed when power is available to the damper actuator. Damper actuator signals are generally from the generator's electrical gear as opposed to the building management system (BMS).

Where acoustical concerns exist, measures may need to be taken both inside the engine/generator room to meet the appropriate OSHA regulations and guidelines (OSHA 1996) and measures may also be required on the air intake/discharge openings should the site be in close proximity to an acoustically sensitive property line.

7.4   BURN-IN ROOMS AND TEST LABS

Many datacom facilities incorporate a dedicated area for the purpose of assembling, configuring, and testing datacom equipment prior to deployment into the production environment. These areas can be used for testing of the equipment power supplies, dual-power capabilities, actual power draw, and cooling requirements, as well as for equipment applications testing (both software and hardware functions).

It is recommended these areas be constructed adjacent to production areas for convenience yet separated with respect to power, cooling, and fire protection to preclude a power or fire system event from affecting the production environment.

7.5   DATACOM EQUIPMENT SPARE PARTS

These areas or rooms should be maintained at the same environmental conditions as the datacom room. The spare parts are most often replacement electronic components. These components often have exposed electrical contact points, making them especially vulnerable to damage from electrostatic discharge (ESD) while being handled. A technician may have need for immediate use of a part for equipment repair. Therefore, the temperature of the space should be similar to that of the operating data center. *Thermal Guidelines for Data Processing Environments* (ASHRAE 2004h) provides allowable temperatures for "product power off" conditions that would include a spare parts room environment.

7.6   STORAGE SPACES

Storage spaces for products such as paper and tapes generally require conditions similar to those in the datacom room. These products expand, contract, or change shape in response to changes in temperature/humidity level, which affects the performance of close-tolerance mechanical devices, such as paper feeders and tape drives.

8

Contamination

8.1   INTRODUCTION

Data processing environment airborne contamination is a potential threat to information technology (IT) equipment reliability and availability. The amount, distribution, and concentration of airborne and settleable contaminants, called *contaminants* throughout this chapter, vary by many factors, including, but not limited to, geographic location, weather, season, outdoor pollutant levels, population influence, building filtration systems as well as maintenance of the systems, and materials used in the data processing environment. Contaminants such as zinc whiskers have generated increased awareness in the data processing environment over the past several years and have been studied extensively. Many papers have been written about contamination problems, controls, and measurements for the telecommunications environment. Standards for IT environment contamination have been published by IEC and Telcordia to better understand and define the installation environment. These standards are well written but are not tailored directly to the data processing environment. IEC 60721-3-3 (IEC 2002) is written with the intent of classifying and specifying environmental parameters and conditions that directly affect the performance of equipment. GR-63-CORE (Telcordia 2002) includes a section on airborne contaminants that provides contamination classes, contamination levels and measurement of contamination levels, test methods, and equipment fan filter criteria for equipment used in telecommunications facilities. Some IT equipment manufacturers have issued contamination guidelines for their equipment, but the general tendency is to make the hardware robust relative to the installation environments that are considered typical. To maximize reliability and availability of IT equipment, it is generally accepted that IT equipment must be installed in data processing installation environments that meet certain guidelines for contamination. The following sections discuss contamination classifications, industry-defined limits for contamination, and design and practices to minimize contaminants.

Thermal Guidelines for Data Processing Environments (ASHRAE 2004h) lists four classes of environments, from class 1 (high-end data centers) to class 4 (point of sale or light industrial environments). This chapter is generally focused on class 1 environments, but the information is beneficial for the users in classes, 2, 3, and 4.

8.2   CONTAMINATION CLASSIFICATIONS

Data processing environments house critical business IT equipment that is dependant on conditioning of the operating environment. Installation planning considerations for operational health typically include power, air conditioning, fire suppression, alarming, and redundancy. Equally important are the detrimental effects of contaminants on IT equipment. In general, contaminants can lead to IT equipment malfunction by invading the equipment and disturbing the equipment's interaction with the environment. Electrical, mechanical, chemical, material, insulation, and thermal failures of IT equipment may be attributed to contamination. For the purpose of this section, contamination is grouped in three general categories:

- Gases
- Solids
- Liquids

The information in this section is intended as a resource for identifying typical sources of contaminants in data processing environments and their potential effects on IT equipment. Each of the contaminant groups is discussed separately, although many have combinations of contaminants that coexist within data processing environments.

8.2.1   Gases

Gaseous contamination is typically controlled sufficiently well by conditioning the air for suitable human occupancy. The following information is not intended to require the facility planner and designer to implement a gaseous monitoring program but, rather, for education.

Two classes of gaseous contamination are corrosive compounds and volatile organics. Corrosion is a complicated electrochemical process occurring when a base metal, corrosion products from the metal, a surface electrolyte such as water, and oxygen from the atmosphere combine (Jones 1992). Corrosion is often dependant on some presence of moisture. Where the temperature and relative humidity are high and the atmospheric compounds are present in sufficient concentration, corrosion may take place on susceptible metal surfaces such as copper or silver. Products of corrosion may cause electrical bridging or shorting of circuits, intermittent electrical leakage, and in extreme cases, open circuits.

Corrosion in an indoor environment is most often initiated by a short list of compounds or combinations of a few compounds. However, there are literally hundreds of compounds that can have a corrosive effect that are not normally found in an indoor environment. Table 8.1 includes the most common and abundant corrosion-inducing compounds that might be found in an indoor data processing environment. The compounds present are highly dependant on the controls put in place to mitigate them.

Table 8.1 Characteristics of Corrosion Initiating Gases

Corrosive Material and Formula	Physical Characteristics	Typical Corrosion Initiators	Typical Industrial Sources
Sulfur Dioxide SO_2	Colorless gas, irritating pungent odor.	Reacts with water to produce highly corrosive sulfuric acid.	Product of combustion of fossil fuel and incineration of organic waste. Also found in paper, fabrics, food preservation, fumigants, and refining.
Hydrogen Sulfide H_2S	Colorless gas, odor of rotten eggs.	Forms metallic sulfides.	Intermediate in chemical synthesis.
Chlorine Cl	Greenish yellow gas, pungent, irritating, choking odor.	Very reactive and produces corrosive metal salts. Combines with all elements except carbon and noble gases.	Widespread use in chemical synthesis, bleaching, oxidant.
Hydrogen Chloride HCl	Colorless, corrosive gas, pungent characteristic odor. Fumes in air.	Quickly soluble in water, reacting to form hydrochloric acid. Corrosion products are copper chloride and other metal salts.	Chlorides and HCl are by-products of coal and incinerator combustion. Widespread use in chemical synthesis, polymers, rubber, and pharmaceuticals.
Nitrogen Dioxide NO_2	Reddish brown gas, suffocating odor.	Highly reactive, forms acid with water. Corrodes electronic materials, forming highly corrosive nitric acid.	Used in chemical synthesis and explosives. Product of combustion from energy production and automobiles.
Ozone O_3	Characteristic pleasant odor in small concentrations.	Most reactive form of oxygen. Found in smog.	Disinfectant for water and air, bleach for textiles, waxes, and oils.
Ammonia NH_3	Colorless, corrosive alkaline gas, pungent odor.	Readily dissolves in water and combines readily with acid gases, producing a corrosive salt.	Refrigeration, fertilizers, synthetic fibers and plastics. Widely used in chemical synthesis.

The corrosive compounds in Table 8.1 are widely used in industry and, in some cases, products of combustion. The compounds are highly reactive, combining readily with metal surfaces directly or with intermediate substances where the combination is responsible for initiating corrosion.

In addition to corrosive compounds, volatile organic compounds (VOCs) may be present in data processing environments. VOCs are carbon-based organic chemical compounds found in or derived from living things (EPA 1990). VOCs vaporize at room temperature and standard barometric pressure. IT equipment is extremely robust against VOCs, although VOCs are most problematic for mechanical switching equipment (Reagor 1985). There are an extraordinary number of VOCs in ordinary air.

8.2.2 Solids

Solids contamination, called *particulates*, exists in a variety of concentrations, size distributions, and compositions. Sources of particulate contamination include, but are not limited to, dust, dirt, lint, hair, skin, soot, ash, shavings, metallic whiskers, and debris. Even a person sitting motionless generates about 100,000 particles per cubic foot per minute (Griner 1994), although most of these particles pose absolutely no threat to IT equipment.

Particulate contamination typically exhibits one or more of the following characteristics: abrasive, hygroscopic, corrosive, conductive, or lower thermal efficiency. These characteristics result in decreased reliability of IT equipment. Abrasive particulates contribute to increased wear and fretting corrosion (van Dijk 1994). Hygroscopic particulates primarily consist of sulfate and nitrate dust. Sulfates and nitrates are water-soluble salts that are of particular concern and are discussed in Telcordia GR-63-CORE. Water-soluble salts have an affinity for moisture and can result in fluctuating contact resistance and bridging or shorting of electrical contacts over time in high relative humidity environments. Most, but not all, water-soluble salts are due to residual contamination on the electrical circuit boards and are not from external sources. Corrosive particulates can result in bridging or shorting failures, as corrosive particulate accumulation, coupled with IT equipment operation in an environment of high relative humidity, can link circuit board patterns or traces. Conductive particulates may be responsible for bridging or shorting two adjacent electrical conductors regardless of the temperature and humidity conditions. Likely candidates of conductive debris are metallic whiskers (tin or zinc) that are dislodged and ejected into the airstream but settle on surfaces rather quickly. IT equipment is vulnerable to particulate contamination in some of the following areas:

- **Air Intake Filters.** Air intake filters, if used, usually have large pores; therefore, the largest particulate contaminants are a problem. Even though the pores are large, dust bunnies (Moore 2003) can form as the larger fibers are trapped on a surface, forming an intertwined network that can trap other matter. Particulates may accumulate in filters and increase resistance to airflow, resulting in lower thermal efficiency or less chilled air reaching the internal components and devices of the equipment. Some IT equipment has thermal protection circuitry to detect overheating and provide warning or shut down before failure.

- **Internal Heat Sinks.** Finned heat sinks on electronic devices are susceptible to particulates clogging the finned structure over time. Accumulation of particulates reduces heat transfer efficiency and may cause the equipment to overheat. This phenomenon is known as thermal fouling (Montgomery 2002). Fouling can also affect power supplies, chassis openings, and internal surfaces in the air circulation path. Particulate deposits reduce convection by blanketing components and devices.

- **Electrical Connectors.** Particulates may be drawn into the contact area and cause electrical failure. However, most connectors have molded housings that preclude any buildup of particulates. Excessive plugging and unplugging of I/O adapters or other interconnects with pins and receptacles can introduce particulates from the surrounding environment or from wear and tear.

- **Removable Media.** Particulate contamination has the potential for damaging or crashing hard disk read/write heads. This is minimized with present hardware as the hard disk read/write heads and storage platters are essentially sealed. Particulate contamination may still present a problem for optical drives or magnetic tape units that have laser or magnetic read/write heads. Physical insertion of media can introduce particulates from the surrounding environment.

Periodic inspection of IT equipment exterior and interior surfaces around the air intake and exhaust locations should be done to look for particulate accumulation.

8.2.3 Liquids

The most notable liquid contamination source found in the data processing environment is water used by chilled-water computer room air conditioners; although other potential sources of water are from humidifiers, condensate (steam condensed back into water), and water-based fire suppression systems. Liquids such as water are generally excellent conductors of electricity and will cause shorting faults at power cord interconnects, communication cable interconnects, and all electronic components, devices, and subsystems installed in the equipment. There are many contaminants that are found in normal water, including, but not limited to, dissolved minerals, bacteria, and silica. Water treatment, if used in air-conditioning or humidification processes, must be done with expert advice and consultation. Mistreated or untreated water can lead to unwanted airborne contaminants. Liquid vapors and mists may also carry corrosive chemicals into IT equipment. Examples include salt fog in coastal areas and aerosol cleaning solutions.

The information provided on gaseous, solids, and liquid contamination is intended to give a fundamental overview of the sources and potential effect on IT equipment. Contamination in specific concentrations or types can affect or degrade the performance of IT equipment. This is recognized by the industry as standards bodies and conglomerations have established limits and methods of test for contaminants. The next section presents the limits and their origins.

8.3 INDUSTRY-DEFINED LIMITS AND TEST METHODS FOR CONTAMINATION IN IT EQUIPMENT ROOMS

Table 8.2 shows a summary of corrosive gas and volatile organic emission limits from IEC and Telcordia. Limits have also been established for many of the same contaminants by the Telecommunications Industry Association (TIA 2004).

The data processing environment most likely belongs to the IE31 set of class combinations in IEC 60721-3-3. According to the standard, IE31 applies to locations continuously temperature-controlled, with heating, cooling, or humidification used where necessary to maintain required conditions. Installed products are exposed to some solar radiation, without particular risk of biological attacks, and in rural or urban areas with low industrial activities, presence of dust or sand minimized, and insignificant vibration and shock. This class combination implies a set of climactic, chemical, biological, and mechanically active (dust-sand) parameters.

Table 8.2 Corrosive Gas and Volatile Organic Industry Limits

Gas	Formula	IEC 60721-3-3	Telcordia GR-63-CORE
Ammonia	NH_3	0.3 mg/m^3 430 ppb	0.348 mg/m^3 500 ppb
Chlorine	CL_2	0.1 mg/m^3 34 ppb	0.014 mg/m^3 5 ppb
Hydrogen chloride	HCL	0.1 mg/m^3 67 ppb	0.007 mg/m^3 5 ppb
Hydrogen sulfide	H_2S	0.01 mg/m^3 7 ppb	0.055 mg/m^3 40 ppb
Ozone	O_3	0.01 mg/m^3 5 ppb	0.245 mg/m^3 125 ppb
Volatile organics	C_nH_n	N.A.	5 mg/m^3 1200 ppb
Sulfur dioxide	SO_2	0.1 mg/m^3 38 ppb	0.131 mg/m^3 50 ppb

ppb = parts per billion
mg/m^3 = milligrams per cubic meter

GR-63-CORE limits used for telecommunications facilities are average yearly levels derived from predictive modeling with particulate filters rated 10% (ASHRAE dust spot efficiency), continuous operation of computer room air-conditioning (CRAC) fans, and supply air composed of 10% outdoor urban environment air and 90% recirculated air.

Table 8.2 does not address occupational areas. There are a number of nationally recognized agencies and organizations that have written industry acceptable guidelines based on protecting human health. For more information on human physiology interaction with corrosive gases and VOCs, consult ASHRAE Standard 62.1-2004, *Ventilation for Acceptable Indoor Air Quality* (ASHRAE 2004j), Occupational Heath and Safety Administration (OSHA), American Conference of Governmental Industrial Hygienists (ACGIH), or National Institute for Occupational Safety and Health (NIOSH).

For solids, there are two basic particulate contamination methods of measurement:

1. Weight measurement/unit volume,
    typically in micrograms per cubic meter ($\mu g/m^3$).
2. Number of particles larger than some size/unit volume,
    typically in number per cubic foot.

There is no direct correlation between the two methods of measurement; however, both methods roughly track each other. For example, when the weight measurement gets larger, the number of solid particulates typically gets larger. Clean room manufacturers establish environments as class 100,000, class 10,000, class 100, etc. These numbers come from Federal Standard 209, first published in 1963 in the US and titled, *Cleanroom and Work Station Requirements, Controlled Environments*. It was revised in 1966 (209A), 1973 (209B), 1987 (209C), 1988 (209D), and 1992 (209E). Federal Standard 209 refers to the number of particles larger than about .5 μm in diameter per cubic foot. Most data processing environment installations would most likely meet class 100,000 if measured in number of particles per unit volume and several might also meet class 20,000. Very few data processing environments are better than class 10,000. Federal Standard 209E has been replaced by International Organization for Standardization (ISO) standards, ISO 14644-1, Part 1, "Classification of Air Cleanliness" (ISO 1999b),and ISO 14644-2, Part 2, specifications for testing and monitoring to prove continued compliance with ISO 14644-1 (ISO 2000).

IT equipment manufacturers do not always specify acceptable particulate contaminant levels for data processing environments. Some manufacturers may comment on particulate contamination by either publishing a filtration requirement or a particulate classification requirement. A typical filtration requirement statement would be:

- Recirculation air systems must be filtered to 40% atmospheric dust spot efficiency according to ASHRAE Standard 52.1 (ASHRAE 1992).
- Outside air must be filtered to 99.97% efficiency or greater. This requires HEPA (high-efficiency particulate air) filters that meet MIL-STD-282. HEPA filters can remove more than 95% of most particulate matter, including particles as small as 0.10-0.20 microns.

Filtering is discussed in further detail in the facility design section.

Particulate classification requirements generally refer to particulate contamination in terms of weight per unit volume and are typically stated in $\mu g/m^3$. For example, the GR-63-CORE requirements, adhered to in Telecommunication installations, specify solid particulate indoor contamination levels as shown in Table 8.3.

The particulate requirements in Table 8.3 are relatively strict requirements and are based on telecommunications experience with particulate contamination in switching facilities. IT hardware manufacturers that specify particulate levels are not as strict in their particulate level requirements.

Test methods and procedures for gaseous and hygroscopic dust contaminants are provided in GR-63-CORE (Telcordia 2002). The gaseous tests are largely based on the American Society for Testing and Materials (ASTM), International Electrotechnical Commission (IEC), and Institute for Electrical and Electronic Engineers (IEEE) standards. GR-1274-CORE is used to perform the hygroscopic dust tests (Telcordia 1994).

Table 8.3 Telecommunication Particulate Contamination and Concentrations

Contaminants	Concentration
Airborne particles (TSP-Dichot 15[a])	20 ug/m^3
Coarse particles	< 10 ug/m^3
Fine particles	15 ug/m^3
Water-soluble salts	10 ug/m^3 max-total
Sulfate	10 ug/m^3
Nitrites	5 ug/m^3
Total	**55 ug/m^3**

[a] TSP-Dichot 15 = total suspended particulates as determined with a dichotomous sampler that has a 15-um inlet.

Liquids do not have any published limits, as the presence of uncontrolled liquid dispersion in the data processing environment is unacceptable.

Standards and technology organizations have established limits for contamination in predefined technology spaces that can be used or extended to IT equipment installed in the data processing environment. While these limits are important, active monitoring is not necessary unless contaminants are suspected in abnormal rates of hardware failures, where factors such as power, air conditioning, or defective parts have been ruled out. The next section discusses methods to minimize contamination and effective, everyday preventive measures that facility planners and designers can implement to control contaminants in the data processing environment.

8.4 FACILITIES DESIGN—GENERAL CONSIDERATIONS FOR DATA PROCESSING ENVIRONMENT INSTALLATIONS

Even though contamination sources are abundant, there are many preventive steps that can be taken to reduce the potential threat to the data processing environment. Facility planners and designers have many options to minimize data processing environment contamination.

8.4.1 Site Selection

Data processing environment site selection, along with identification of surrounding internal and external hazards, is an important consideration. Neighbors with agricultural, chemical, biological, nuclear, or manufacturing processes and storage, geographical locations that are prone to floods, volcanoes, or other acts by Mother Nature, proximity to an airport and the flight path of planes, etc., can put the data processing environment at risk. The data processing environment should be physically separate from space continuously occupied by humans and located within a building away from potential local hazards. For example, operations such as cafeterias or toilets located above the data processing environment and boiler rooms or parking garages located below can negatively affect the data processing environment contaminant level in the event of an accident or act of terrorism. In some instances, a high-risk location cannot be avoided.

8.4.2 Construction

A new data processing environment is erected and usually sufficiently cleaned to minimize construction debris prior to infrastructure and IT equipment installation. However, environments are renovated or expanded to accommodate the increasing data processing needs of the clients. Construction materials and processes have a huge impact on the quantity of contaminants that may be present in the environment. Interior walls, usually made from sheetrock or gypsum board, and the installation process (e.g., mudding, taping, sanding) can release a significant amount of dust and debris into the environment that can easily find its way into IT equipment. The materials used for paint and preparation, especially if organic solvent-based, can outgas

VOCs. The sources of VOCs are too numerous to list, but other typical sources are building insulation material, adhesives, upholstery, plastic compounds, rubber compounds, and carpeting.

8.4.3 Fire Prevention

Fire prevention techniques vary by data processing environment, usually at the direction of the insurance provider or authority having jurisdiction (e.g., fire marshall). Many data processing environments use some type of fluorocarbon-based fire suppressant, but some facilities use water mist fire suppressant systems. With fluorocarbon-based systems, no IT equipment damage should occur and no subsequent equipment cleanup is required unless there is fire-related damage. Water-based systems are a proven method to extinguish fires; however, water can impact IT equipment reliability and availability. Since IT equipment complies with product safety agency standards that require IT equipment to be designed with a minimum amount of consumable, self-extinguishing material (UL 2001a), facility planners and designers should take steps to ensure that the IT equipment is not directly exposed to water in a fire situation. Ideally, the sprinkler system should be designed to prevent the water from coming in direct contact or entrained into the IT equipment by air-moving devices (AMDs) such as fans and blowers. If allowable by codes governing the data processing environment, subject to interpretation by the authority having jurisdiction (AHJ), protective covers should be installed over the IT equipment to prevent water damage, especially upon accidental discharge of the water mist fire suppressant system. However, even with protective covers, liquid infiltration is still possible if the AMDs are operating (if electrical power has not been removed by an emergency power off).

8.4.4 Raised-Floor Design

A majority of data processing environments utilize a raised floor. The raised floor is used to protect the electrical and communications cabling to the IT equipment without impacting the ability to walk in the vicinity of the hardware as well as to minimize abrasion to the cables. A raised floor also acts as a way to deliver chilled air through perforated panels to the IT equipment. The floor-to-ceiling airflow pattern takes advantage of the natural buoyancy of the IT equipment's hot exhaust air. Additionally, the raised-floor panels are part of electrostatic discharge (ESD) control. With a conducting bottom surface in contact with floor stringers and pedestals that are part of the facility grounding path, it is possible to make a signal plane that can conduct electromagnetic emissions and ESD discharges to ground. The conducting bottom surface of the raised-floor panels is typically a plated sheet metal. The plating can be a source of metallic debris called a whisker. These whiskers are typically zinc (Zn), but occasionally they can be tin (Sn). If the whiskers are dislodged and carried in the chilled airstream underneath the raised floor, it is possible for the suspended whisker to exit through a perforated panel, enter, and settle in the IT equipment. The result may be arcing and bridging or shorting of components such as transistors in IT equipment power supplies. Design practices for raised-floor panels, stringers, pedestals, and underfloor fixtures (e.g., cable trays, drip pans) are as follows:

- Wrought aluminum sheet is suitable for raised-floor panels and structures. Wrought aluminum alloys can also be used for the risers and stanchions if the strength of the aluminum parts is adequate for the load.
- Galvanneal (a Zn coating applied to steel by a hot dip process followed by a heat treatment) is suitable for use in raised-floor structures. It is necessary to ensure that the path to ground meets the electrical requirements. Sometimes a ground strap is needed with galvanneal to ensure good electrical contact with ground. The facility planners and designers should be careful not to get electrogalvanneal, which is susceptible to whisker problems.
- Stainless steel is suitable for raised-floor structures provided that the electrical path to ground meets the electrical requirements.
- Steel with an electroplated Zn or Sn plating should not be utilized without expert materials advice. These plating materials are the primary source of whiskers in IT equipment installations.
- Aluminized steel (steel with an aluminum coating applied by immersion of the steel in a molten aluminum bath) is too soft for an acceptable raised-floor installation. Debris will form with the removal and reinstallation of the raised-floor panels.
- Conductive paints should not be used as a surface finish on the underside sheet metal. The conductive paint will not prevent whisker growth if the base sheet metal is susceptible to whisker growth.
- Tin-plated metal should be avoided. Tin whiskers will grow on electroplated tin surfaces.

Expert advice and consultation should be sought for proper choice of raised-floor panels, stringers, pedestals, and underfloor infrastructure.

Carpeting in data processing environments is a source of particulate contamination as well as VOCs and should be avoided when possible. Loose carpet fibers can easily become airborne and act as bridges between electrical components or clog filters due to their large surface to mass ratio. Some carpeting may contain carbon or other conductive fibers to ensure ESD requirements are maintained. The materials in the carpeting can also release various types of organic chemical vapors, some of which may be harmful to IT equipment. Most IT equipment is currently designed to be reasonably robust to these types of organic chemical vapors. Nevertheless, the facility planners and designers should seek expert advice in the choice of any carpeting or rubber matting material.

After choosing the appropriate materials for the floor, the location of perforated panels is considered. To maximize delivery of chilled air, the common practice is to place perforated panels directly in front of or underneath IT equipment as required by the IT equipment manufacturers. However, the rising chilled airstream through the raised-floor perforated panels can carry particulates from under the raised floor or on top of the raised floor into the IT equipment via the AMDs. The faster the air is exiting from the raised-floor panels, the more propensity it has to carry a larger number and mass of contaminants. If the manufacturer requires locating perforated panels directly in front of IT equipment, it is necessary to take additional precautions relative to underfloor contamination sources. For example, the subfloor should be sealed to prevent the dusting of concrete and cleaned periodically to prevent particulate buildup.

8.4.5 Overhead Supply Air

Discharge air from ceiling diffusers, typically used in non-raised-floor environments, should not introduce contaminants. Particulates in the ductwork can drop down and be pulled into the IT equipment via the AMDs. If it is not possible to eliminate ceiling-mounted diffusers, these diffusers should not be located directly over IT equipment. If it is absolutely necessary to locate a supply air diffuser above IT equipment, other provisions should be considered. For example, the air-conditioning ductwork should not be connected to air-conditioning ductwork that services building areas other than the data processing environment. The opportunity for cross-contamination is very high if the building ductwork is interconnected. Access points in the air-conditioning ductwork should be provided to permit easy cleaning operations. Thorough cleaning of ductwork must be performed after construction is complete but prior to facility operations. If ducting is located above IT equipment, careful, periodic cleaning is highly recommended.

8.4.6 Ceiling Panels

Ceiling panels for new installations or replacements should have an impervious surface. Existing ceiling panels in suspended ceilings should be tested for particulate generation. Shake the ceiling panel and look for particulates that flake. A bright light is useful for examining these particles. There are no published standards for ceiling panels, but the facility planners and designers should insist on a review of the ceiling panel material and the acceptance criteria should be zero particles generated via a shake test. A good ceiling grid design uses gypsum panels with a vinyl covering to eliminate particulates.

8.4.7 Temperature and Humidity Control

Temperature and humidity impact the reliability and the rate of corrosion in a data processing environment. Precision computer room air conditioning is critical for IT equipment installations since most IT equipment is air cooled. The air-conditioning temperature and humidity requirements are dependant on the class of equipment defined in *Thermal Guidelines for Data Processing Environments* (ASHRAE

2004h). Temperature control has an impact on reliability. Too high a temperature sustained for a period of time shortens the mean time between failure (MTBF) of transistors and capacitors. Temperature cycling, which affects connectors and solder joints by repeated expansion and contraction, also results in varying relative humidity. Too high a relative humidity may lead to condensation and, thus, acceleration of corrosion if corrosive compounds or VOCs are present, and too low a relative humidity could lead to ESD damage. Good temperature and relative humidity control should incorporate constant monitoring devices to record real-time temperature and relative humidity data in several areas of the data processing environment. Excursions should be noted.

8.4.8   Filtration

Some degree of air filtering is necessary in data processing environments. Filtering make take place in recirculated air via the computer room air-conditioning units, in makeup air supplied from the outside environment, and in some IT equipment. Two ASHRAE filter standards are currently used, Standard 52.1-1992 (ASHRAE 1992) and Standard 52.2-1999 (ASHRAE 1999), to rate filters based on their collection efficiency, pressure drop, and particulate-holding capacity. Standard 52.1-1992 measures arrestance, dust spot efficiency, and dust holding capacity. *Arrestance* is a measure of a filter's ability to capture a mass fraction of coarse dust, and *dust spot efficiency* is the ability to capture particles within a given size range. Standard 52.2-1999 measures particle size efficiency expressed as a minimum efficiency reporting value (MERV) between 1 and 20. Table 8.4 shows a comparison of the ASHRAE standards.

Particulate filters with a 20%-30% ASHRAE 52.1 dust spot rating are commonly available for computer room air-conditioning (CRAC) units (Liebert 2003). However, internal to the CRAC units, loose or misaligned blower belts can create metallic content particulates not filtered by CRACs. There are specialized belt products that minimize this problem. The use of variable-frequency drives or electronically commutated motors (EC motors) could also be used to eliminate the use of belts and associated contamination. CRAC belt drives should be precision aligned and checked frequently. Higher efficiency filtration may be necessary for some data processing environment installations. The presence of significant concentrations of VOCs may require activated charcoal and permanganate-based filters to reduce VOCs to an acceptable level.

Filtration invariably impedes the airflow through the air-conditioning system and IT equipment; thus, it is important for the design to take the filter impedance into account. Filters should be inspected and replaced or cleaned at regularly defined intervals to minimize airflow impedance. Some equipment uses active alarming based on differential pressure drop to indicate when filters need to be serviced, as manufacturer-defined time intervals may not be accurate due to variations in or severity of environmental conditions. IT equipment, especially for the telecommu-

Table 8.4   Comparison of ASHRAE 52.1 and 52.2 Standards

	ASHRAE 52.2			ASHRAE 52.1		
MERV	3-10 µm	1-3 µm	0.3-1 µm	Arrestance	Dust Spot	Dust Spot
1	<20%	-	-	<65%	<20%	
2	<20%	-	-	65-70%	<20%	>10 µm
3	<20%	-	-	70-75%	<20%	
4	<20%	-	-	>75%	<20%	
5	20-35%	-	-	80-85%	<20%	
6	35-50%	-	-	>90%	<20%	3.0-10 µm
7	50-70%	-	-	>90%	20-25%	
8	>70%	-	-	>95%	25-30%	
9	>85%	<50%	-	>95%	40-45%	
10	>85%	50-65%	-	>95%	50-55%	1.0-3.0 µm
11	>85%	65-80%	-	>98%	60-65%	
12	>90%	>80%	-	>98%	70-75%	
13	>90%	>90%	<75%	>98%	80-90%	
14	>90%	>90%	75-85%	>98%	90-95%	0.3-1.0 µm
15	>90%	>90%	85-95%	>98%	~95%	
16	>95%	>95%	>95%	>98%	>95%	
17*	>99%	>99%	>99%	-	>99%	
18*	>99%	>99%	>99%	-	>99%	0.3-1.0 µm
19*	>99%	>99%	>99%	-	>99%	
20*	>99%	>99%	>99%	-	>99%	

* Filters viruses and carbon dust

nications industry, is fitted with filters that have a minimum dust arrestance of 80% (10%-51% ASHRAE dust spot efficiency) as outlined by GR-63-CORE. Data processing environments are dependant on proper air filtration and maintenance to achieve proper airflow and equipment performance.

8.4.9   Positive Pressurization

Positive pressurization with outside air is used to keep particulate contaminants out of the data processing environment as well as control corrosive gases and VOCs (Krzyzanowski 1991). Even though most installations in typical commercial business and clean industrial locations have adequate quality of surrounding air, any air entering the data processing environment should be conditioned and filtered to ensure it is within specifications for IT equipment temperature, humidity, and cleanliness. Fresh makeup air is also a code requirement for IT equipment installations with human occupants. Typical fresh air exchange rates are in the range of 0.5-1.5 air changes per hour (ACH) and higher if air-side economizers are used. The typical installation has minimal filtration of the outside air before allowing the makeup air into the data processing environment. If data processing environments do not filter the outside air, the data processing environment is essentially contaminated with all the pollutants present. This practice can be disastrous to IT equipment if the outside air is heavily polluted. Outside air in all geographic locations has its own peculiarities relative to pollution. While it is advisable to have makeup air enter the data processing environment for positive pressurization to minimize the influx of office particulates, the design of the fresh air makeup should be designed with the same degree of prudence as for the air conditioning. Successful makeup air system design must provide positive pressurization with low maintenance and low acoustic noise (Frank 1994).

8.4.10 IT Equipment Installation

Pre-installation activities that involve fabrication of cables or other parts should be done outside the data processing environment. Wire snipping and termination of connectors on communications or power cables can shed insulation fibers and metal shavings. Forming and fitting of support structures, as well as drilling, filing, sanding, use of cutting fluids (oil-based and chemical), etc., can load the environment with gaseous, particulate, and liquid contaminants.

Although not always considered, IT equipment itself is a minor contributor to contamination. IT equipment has a chemical emissions profile, including VOCs, but IT chemical emission rates are directly dependant upon the materials and solvents used in manufacture of the product, internal operating temperatures, and the chemical nature of the supplies or media used in the product under normal operating conditions. Printers, copiers, and tape media are possible sources of contamination that can impact operations of other types of IT equipment. Advancements in materials and technology have somewhat eliminated the concern over printers, copiers, and tape media, but care should be taken when planning the installation. It is recommended that printers, copiers, and tape media be placed in separate areas with separate air-handling arrangements to prevent any cross-contamination. If data processing space is limited and it is not possible to separate printers, copiers, and tape media from other equipment, it may be necessary to make other arrangements. Printers are a source of paper and toner dust, silicone oils, aluminum particles, and VOCs. Exhaust air via a hood or other methods are possible solutions, but negative pressurization of the data processing environment must be avoided for contaminant control (Krzyzanowski 1991). Laser printers that use a hot filament technique are potential ozone generators, but emissions are below acceptable health limits. Copiers that use wet and dry processes each have their own risks from oily carbon particles and carbon toner particles, respectively (Reagor 1985). Tape drives may generate a particular type of debris called iron fibers or iron whiskers. These iron-rich tape media fibers are iron particles that are encased in an oxide layer and then imbedded in the tape polymer; therefore, they are not conductive. These fibers are nontoxic and do not pose any threat to IT equipment or personnel. These fibers are typically 5-10 mm long and about 2-3 microns (120 micro inches) in diameter.

Directly cooled rack enclosures, especially those that are sealed and utilize a closed architecture, can permit additional isolation from the ambient environment and contaminants.

8.4.11 Operational Strategies

The most effective method to deal with contaminants is to keep them out of the data processing environment. Data processing environment practices should be written to minimize contaminants carried in by everyday occurrences. Absolutely no food or drink should be allowed in the data processing environment at any time. Crumbs from food or spilled liquids put IT equipment at risk. Cardboard boxes and IT equipment manuals should remain outside the data processing environment in a designated location. Paper is a particulate source as well as a fuel source in the event of a fire. A staging area should be sought to remove IT equipment from boxes and packaging prior to entering the data processing environment. It is vital for the facility planners and designers to designate a staging area for unpacking and the moving in/ moving out of IT equipment. Tacky pads or sticky mats should be installed just beyond the entrance(s) to the data processing environment to remove debris from shoes. Positive pressurization via conditioned makeup air, air showers, or vestibules are possible options for reducing the influx of contaminants.

Raised floor and subfloor cleaning is necessary to keep contamination under control. However, cleaning should only be done by qualified professionals with experience. Specialized companies use techniques and equipment designed to clean without introducing contaminants back into the data processing environment or disturbing IT equipment operation. However, cleaning is subject to some risk from human error. For example, power and network connections that are not secure could be accidentally disconnected, Zn or Sn whiskers can flake from the raised-floor panels when moved, or fire suppression systems could accidentally be triggered. While using professionals is recommended, if cleaning must be done by facility personnel, the products used must be anti-static, noncorrosive, as well as odor- and residue-free. Only vacuums with HEPA filters and brooms, and mops approved for the data processing environment should be allowed.

IT equipment cleaning should be done only at the IT manufacturers' direction using specified tools, techniques, and solvents. IT equipment cleaning is not an ordinary operation as is office cleaning.

A liquid-detection method should be used to alarm in the event of a water leak. Some data processing environments use trenches for water supply and return lines to the computer room air-conditioning units. In the event of a leak, water is contained with the trenches. IT equipment components, devices, subsystems, and interconnects cannot survive submersion in liquid for extended periods of time. Commonly used watertight power connectors that conform to IP67 (International Electrotechnical Commission 2001) are dustproof and offer protection from temporary immersion in water 1 meter deep for 30 minutes.

8.4.12 Site Survey

Environmental reviews and audits can be conducted by professionals where gaseous, particulate, and liquid contaminants or a combination of the three is suspected as contributing to IT equipment failures. On-site measurements along with laboratory analysis provide answers to potential sources of contaminants and corrective actions to mitigate their impact. Literature is available that outlines collection methodology and techniques, but there are consulting firms and IT equipment manufacturers that specialize in this type of work (Krzyzanowski 1991; Osborne 1996).

8.5 SUMMARY

Potential contamination sources exist everywhere and are unavoidable in any building, structure, or technology space, including data processing. Contaminants, in the form of gases, solids, and liquids, may be hazardous to IT equipment operational health if not considered adequately. The background information on gaseous, solid, and liquid contamination, as well as limits and references to limits set by agencies and organizations, are provided for awareness. While there are a lot of items to consider, strategies can be put in place to efficiently and effectively minimize the threat of contaminants. Prior to design and construction, site selection is critical for long-term survival of IT equipment in the data processing environment. During the design and construction phase of a data processing environment, materials selection of everything from the raised floor to the ceiling should be chosen to minimize contamination. Important decisions must be made as to pressurization, introduction of outside air, and finishes. Infrastructure equipment selection, installation, and maintenance, as well as IT equipment placement, have an effect on the long-term cleanliness of the data processing environment once it is in day-to-day use. Operations strategies and policies must be clear and understood by all personnel to keep contaminants out of the data processing environment. Prevention of equipment-threatening contaminants is vital to reliability and availability of IT equipment. If there is a reason to believe that there is a significant presence of gaseous, particulate, or liquid contaminants in the data processing environment, an IT equipment manufacturer or qualified professional should be sought to determine the type of contaminant and whether or not it is in a high enough concentration to harm the IT equipment. The identification of possible contaminants and practical mitigation methods should be used extensively to manage unwanted data processing environment contamination.

9

Acoustical Noise Emissions

9.1   ACOUSTICS

Acoustical noise emissions in datacom facilities are a combination of the noise emissions from the datacom equipment itself, as well as the noise emissions from the HVAC equipment used to provide the facility with air conditioning. The noise level of air-cooled datacom equipment has generally been increasing along with the power density and heat loads, so this is an important issue for datacom facility planners and equipment manufacturers alike. Densely populated datacom facilities may run the risk of exceeding OSHA noise limits (and thus potentially causing hearing damage unless personnel are provided with hearing protection) and reference should be made to the appropriate OSHA regulations and guidelines (OSHA 1996). European occupational noise limits are somewhat more stringent than OSHA's and are mandated in EC Directive 2003/10/EC (European Council 2003). Facility noise level calculations can be made following the methodology outlined in the "Sound and Vibration" chapter of *ASHRAE Fundamentals* (ASHRAE 2005c). An acoustical consultant may be needed to properly predict sound levels from multiple sources and paths, as is typically the case in a datacom facility.

In the past, the issue of acoustical noise levels in datacom facilities may not have been an issue of particular concern to data center managers or planners. There are at least two reasons for this. First, the noise levels of the individual datacom products on the floor were not noticeably high, and, second, data centers of the past were mostly in isolated "back room" areas where only a few operators or service personnel might have been located for relatively short periods of time. Certain trends over the last decade or so, however, have made the problem of excessive noise levels in data centers an important one for data center planners and equipment manufacturers alike. These trends include: (1) the packaging of higher and higher performance electronics, such as microprocessors, memory, and control logic into smaller and smaller modules; (2) the ability to package more and more of these modules into a standard-sized datacom rack, cabinet, or frame; (3) the desire to install as many of these racks, cabinets, and frames as possible over the available floor area, often "brick-walling" them across the length and width of the floor; (4) the resultant need for more computer room air-conditioning units or other cooling equipment to keep the datacom equipment running; and (5) the desire in some companies to proudly display their high-tech data centers to visitors or to locate employees and other personnel in the data center area itself. The first and second trends are responsible for the increase in the acoustical noise levels of the individual datacom racks themselves. The denser packaging of the electronics has caused dramatic increases in heat load density with an attendant demand for much greater cooling airflow through the individual rack modules and the overall rack itself. The principal sources of noise in datacom equipment are the air-moving devices (fans, blowers, motorized impellers) and the more airflow required, the more noise. The third trend, the higher density of installed equipment, further compounds the problem because not only are the individual datacom racks noisier but there are more of them on the floor. If two racks now occupy the same floor space taken up by one of them in the past, the noise level to which a person on the floor would be exposed will double. And if each rack were now twice as noisy as in the past, the noise level will be doubled yet again.

The fourth trend, which is a direct result of the increased heat load density of the equipment installed on the data center floor, is responsible for a further increase in the noise levels in the data center. The acoustical noise level of a typical computer room air-conditioning unit is invariably much higher than a typical datacom equipment rack. In the past, when there might have been only a few of these units, spaced well apart and located at the far end or along the perimeter of the floor, their higher noise levels were not a significant factor since there were so few of them compared to the number of datacom products on the floor. Today, however, not only are there many more air-conditioning units in the typical data center, but they are being installed throughout the floor space. Again, the result is that employees, visitors, and other personnel may now be exposed to higher noise levels on the data center floor than in the past.

The fifth trend, that of locating personnel in the data center, does not contribute to higher noise levels, of course, but makes the issue of data center noise levels more acute and in need of attention. Clearly, if human beings could be totally isolated from the datacom facility noise levels, there would be no problem. It is only when they are physically exposed to the noise that it becomes an issue, and the issue may be one of either safety and health or of employee comfort and productivity, as identified below.

9.2   ASHRAE RESOURCES

It is not the intent of this section to address the issue of data center acoustical noise or its control in any technical depth but, rather, to give a broad overview of the problem. For the interested reader, the "Sound and Vibration" chapter of *ASHRAE Fundamentals* (ASHRAE 2005c) provides a good background on some of the basic issues in acoustics and noise control that might be helpful in understanding the problem of data center noise and its control. There is also the "Sound and Vibration Control" chapter in the *ASHRAE Handbook—HVAC Applications* (ASHRAE 2003e) that discusses in more practical terms the noise from mechanical equipment and HVAC systems and provides some guidelines for noise control. However, neither of these chapters deals specifically with datacom facilities themselves or the particular types of IT equipment and air-conditioning units that are typically found in these facilities. For data center managers and planners who are, or may be, faced with an excessive noise problem, the services of a qualified acoustical consultant may be required to solve or ameliorate the problem. A good starting point for finding a suitable consultant is the Web site for the National Council of Acoustical Consultants (http://www.ncac.com). General information about the field of noise control engineering, as well as many useful links and contacts, may be found on the Web site of the Institute of Noise Control Engineering (http://www.inceusa.org).

9.3 THREE ASPECTS OF THE NOISE PROBLEM: THE SOURCE, PATH, AND RECEIVER

A source of noise emits a certain amount of sound energy into the environment or room in which it is located. This is true whether or not there are people in the room to receive (or hear) this energy or, if there are, where they are located or how far away from the source they are. It is also true regardless of what happens to the sound after it is emitted from the source or whether or not there are other noise sources in the room also emitting sound. Thus, the sound emitted by the noise source is used to quantify the source itself, independent of the subsequent transmission and reception of the sound, and the term *emission* is applied to this aspect of the overall noise problem. The sound emitted may be characterized by its amplitude, frequency content, temporal variations, and directionality. The amplitude of the noise emitted by a sound source is quantified in terms of its *sound power level*, in either decibels (dB) or bels (B).

As the sound radiates away from the noise source, it may be reflected by walls and other obstacles in its path; it may be partially absorbed by the reflecting surfaces; it may be partially transmitted through the surfaces it strikes; and it may be scattered by, or diffracted around, the obstacles in its path. All of these are aspects of the *transmission* of sound, and each depends not only on the frequency content of the sound but also on the characteristics of the surfaces and obstacles it strikes. It is a very complex task to analyze what happens to the sound as it bounces around even the simplest of rooms.

The third aspect of the problem is the *reception* of sound, usually by a human being, but in some cases by a microphone or other recording device. The term *immission* (pronounced "eye-mission") is often used to denote this aspect, to complement the use of *emission* at the source end. Contrary to the emission of sound by the source, the immission of sound at the listener's ear *does* depend on the other noise sources in the room, the location of the listener in the room, the geometry of the room and characteristics of its surfaces, as well as many other factors. The sound received by a listener is usually characterized by its amplitude, frequency content, and temporal variations. As opposed to the noise emission from a source, the amplitude of the noise received by a listener is quantified in terms of its *sound pressure level*, in decibels (dB).

From the perspective of data center managers and planners, ultimate concern should be focused on the noise exposure of their employees, visitors, or other personnel in the data center—how loud is the noise, how long are they exposed, are they at risk of hearing damage, how is the noise interfering with their jobs or comfort, etc.? In this regard, the *sound pressure levels* that exist at various points in the datacom facility are of primary interest and should be measured and monitored. On the other hand, the main contributors to the sound pressure level in the room are the individual noise sources, so the *sound power levels* of the individual datacom racks, room air-conditioning units, and auxiliary equipment should also be of concern and should be reduced if possible. The lower the sound power levels of these individual pieces of equipment, the lower will be the sound pressure levels in the room. Information on the sound power levels of the equipment installed in the data center can usually be obtained from the product manufacturers. Finally, the transmission path may also be an important issue to data center managers. Installing absorptive materials on the walls or ceiling, prudently locating sound-attenuating screens and panels, or simply rearranging the equipment layout with respect to personnel work areas may be significant in reducing the sound pressure levels at listeners' ears (even when the source emission levels remain the same).

9.4   THE EFFECTS OF NOISE ON PEOPLE

There are two categories of effects that acoustical noise can have on people: auditory (or physiological) effects and nonauditory (or nonphysiological) effects. Auditory effects include hearing damage, in all of its forms. Hearing damage occurs when the noise level at the ear (noise immission) is very high or when the exposure is over a long period of time. From an employer's perspective, potential hearing damage is a serious issue, not only from the employee's health perspective, but also from the risk of law suits, regulatory fines, and negative publicity. Good sources for background information on the causes of and protection against hearing damage are the National Institute for Occupational Safety and Health and their Web site: http://www.cdc.gov/niosh/topics/noise/ and the World Health Organization and their guidelines and publications (WHO 2004). Nonauditory effects include annoyance, stress, diminished productivity and concentration, and interference with communication. Although not as serious as hearing damage, these "human factor" issues can negatively affect business due to lowered job satisfaction and motivation. A good source for background on the nonauditory effects of noise can be found in USEPA (1981), available at: http://www.nonoise.org/library/handbook/handbook.htm/, and an informative audio CD demonstrating some of the consequences of excessive noise in a workplace is available from NASA (Nelson 2003). In terms of today's datacom facilities, most of the problems associated with complaints about excessive noise will be those in the nonauditory category, particularly annoyance. However, in some large data centers, where datacom racks are lined up side by side over the entire floor and where a relatively large number of air-conditioning units are required for cooling, the sound pressure levels may be high enough to cause hearing damage (see below for more information on this).

9.5 THE SOUND POWER LEVEL OF A NOISE SOURCE

Clearly, the most effective way to reduce the sound pressure levels in a room containing datacom equipment is to reduce the sound power levels of the individual sources. This "source noise control" is always the first approach to a noise control problem and any noise control engineer or acoustical consultant will focus on this from the start. Secondarily, approaches dealing with the path (acoustical absorption, screens, etc.) should be attempted, and only as a last resort should noise control at the receiver (hearing protectors, isolation, rotating shifts, etc.) be looked at. The sound power level is defined as follows:

$$L_W = 10\log\left(W/W_0\right)$$

where

L_W = sound power level, decibels (dB)

W = sound power emitted, watts (W)

W_0 = reference sound power, internationally agreed upon as 10^{-12} W

The sound power level of a source cannot be measured directly but must be determined from measurements of the sound pressure level at many points around the source, usually with the source installed in a special acoustical environment, such as a hemi-anechoic chamber or reverberation room. The sound power radiated by a source is a function of frequency, and engineers generally measure L_W in individual frequency bands, such as one-third octave bands. However, to be able to use a convenient single-number descriptor to characterize the overall sound power level (or the sound pressure level, for that matter), several standardized "frequency weightings" have been internationally agreed upon. These are frequency-response characteristics, or "curves," that are applied to the raw data so that the data may be summed over frequency to yield a single number that represents the overall level.

By far the most common is the "A-weighting" frequency response curve. This curve weights the data to approximate how a human ear would respond to the sound, generally attenuating the levels at the lower frequencies where the ear is less sensitive (see ASHRAE [2005c] for more information). To indicate an A-weighted level, the subscript A is added to the symbol: L_{WA} for the A-weighted sound power level. Specifications for the noise emission levels of products, as well as the "declared" noise levels available to the public, are stated in terms of the A-weighted sound power level. To clearly distinguish between sound power levels and sound pressure levels (a common source of confusion), the former are usually stated in bels (B) rather than decibels (dB). This is particularly true in the information technology industry, where the A-weighted sound power levels of IT products are given in bels. (*Note*: Sound pressure levels are never given in bels, only decibels.)

A major component of the sound power level of IT equipment originates from the air-moving devices needed to provide cooling (fans, blowers, motorized impellers). Air-moving device noise is closely intertwined with the thermal design of the package because the sound power level of the fan or blower depends on the required airflow, backpressure, air-moving device type and operating point, and especially the details of the inlet conditions (airflow uniformity, turbulence ingestion, etc.). A joint thermal-acoustical approach to IT equipment design is essential. Fortunately, this is being facilitated as practical engineering information on air-moving devices becomes easier to obtain from the manufacturers and suppliers.

9.6   LIMITS ON THE SOUND POWER LEVELS OF DATACOM EQUIPMENT

Acoustical noise limits for individual products to be installed in typical data centers have been endorsed by the Information Technology Industry Council (http://www.itic.org/). Limits are given for a wide range of equipment intended for different environments (the data processing area being one). The noise emission limits are given in terms of statistical upper limit A-weighted sound power levels (or "declared" A-weighted sound power level) and are published in the Swedish "Statskontoret" regulation that has become the de facto standard for the worldwide IT industry (see Sweden 2004), available at http://www.statskontoret.se/upload/2619/TN26-6.pdf). The noise emission limits were selected to ensure that the resulting sound pressure levels in the applicable environment would not be excessive. As an example, the declared A-weighted sound power level for an individual computer rack or frame with a footprint of 1 m^2 or less and intended for "generally attended data processing areas" should not exceed 7.5 B. The "declared" value (as opposed to a measured, or mean, value) represents a statistical upper limit for the sound power level below which a stated large percentage (in this case, 93.5%) of the product noise emission levels can be expected to fall with a high degree of confidence (in this case, 95%). For more information on the use of statistical upper limits for noise emission declarations, see ISO 7574 [ISO 1985]). The information technology industry has developed its own internationally standardized test codes for measuring the noise emission levels of its products: ISO 7779 (ISO 1999a), ECMA 74 (ECMA 2003), as well as a test code for uniformly declaring and verifying the noise emission levels, ISO 9296 (ISO 1988). In view of this, noise emission levels of most IT equipment installed or planning to be installed in a datacom facility should be available from the IT manufacturer.

The manufacturers of chillers and other air-conditioning units for datacom facilities, unfortunately, have not been as active as the IT industry in terms of attention to noise control or the development of industry test codes. As a result, the noise emission levels of computer room air-conditioning equipment are generally higher (on an equivalent floor area basis) than the IT products that populate the data center. Furthermore, lacking industry test codes for uniform noise declaration procedures, it is difficult to obtain the sound power level information for these types of products. This situation is expected to change in the coming years as the need for data center cooling increases and the number of air-conditioning units on the floor increases proportionately. The overall noise level in the data center may then be governed by the air-conditioning equipment, not the IT equipment, and perhaps there will be more pressure on the industry to lower its product noise levels.

9.7   THE SOUND PRESSURE LEVEL IN A ROOM

The sound pressure level that exists at any point in a datacom facility results from an accumulation of the sound energy from all the noise sources in the room. This includes noise that may be radiating from overhead HVAC ducts as well as noise that radiates from underfloor cooling, through perforated floor tiles. As mentioned above, this level is affected not only by the strength of each source but by the physical arrangement of the products on the floor and the sound reflective and absorptive characteristics of the room surfaces and the surfaces of the products and other objects in the room.

The sound pressure level is defined at a point in space as follows:

$$Lp = 10\log (p^2 / p_0^2)$$

where

L_p = sound pressure level, decibels (dB)

p = root-mean-square sound pressure at a point, pascals (Pa)

p_0 = reference sound pressure, internationally agreed upon as 20 μPa

As opposed to the sound power level discussed above, the sound pressure level *can* be measured directly, and rather easily, using a sound level meter. These are available in many types and ranges of sophistication, but a basic, relatively inexpensive model is good enough to allow a data center manager or industrial hygienist to get an idea of what the typical sound pressure levels in the room are and where the problem areas might be. Sound pressure level is also a function of frequency and is often measured in frequency bands such as one-third octave bands. The comments above relating to the A-weighting curve apply to sound pressure level as well, and it is the A-weighted sound pressure level, L_{pA}, that is most commonly measured and stated.

Although the sound pressure level at a particular receiver location in a room is *related* to the sound power levels of the noise sources in that room, the relationship is complicated and depends on many factors. These include the number of sound sources, the relative levels of each source, the distance of each source to the receiver, the directivity of each source, the acoustical absorption properties of the walls, floors, ceiling, and obstacles in the room, and the reflection and scattering of the sound from the equipment and other obstacles in the room. If the data center already exists and is operational, it is no problem to simply measure the sound pressure levels at various locations in the room. However, if major changes are being proposed or a new data center is being planned, the services of an acoustical consultant or the use of a commercial software package will most likely be needed to make predictions of the sound pressure levels. The sound *power* levels of the individual pieces of data-com equipment will be needed to make such predictions, and manufacturers should have that information available for their products. Regardless of the complexity of the prediction problem, however, one thing is clear: the higher the sound power levels of the equipment in the room, the higher will be the resulting sound pressure levels. Thus, selecting IT equipment or air-conditioning equipment with the lowest sound power levels at the outset is the most prudent approach to low-noise data center planning.

The following simplified formula may be used to provide a general idea of how the *sound pressure level* at a point in the data center can be estimated from the *sound power level* of a source.

$$L_p = L_W + 10\log_{10}\left(\frac{1}{2\pi r^2} + \frac{4}{R}\right)$$

where L_p is the sound pressure level at a particular receiver location in the room (either the A-weighted level or the level in a particular frequency band), L_W is the sound power level of the source, r is the distance from the source to the receiver, and R is the so-called *room constant* of the space: $R = \alpha/(1-\alpha)$, where α is the average sound absorption coefficient of the surfaces of the room, including those of the installed equipment (typical values are available in the literature, such as Harris [1994]).

In practice, there are many sources in the room, and this equation is modified as follows to take this into account:

$$L_p = L_W + 10\log_{10}\left(\sum_i 10^{0.1L_{Wi}}\left(\frac{1}{2\pi r_i^2} + \frac{4}{R}\right)\right)$$

where L_{Wi} is the sound power level of the *i*th source and r_i its distance to the receiver. The first term in parentheses accounts for "direct" sound that travels directly from a source to the receiver, and the second term accounts for "reverberant" sound, which reflects from room surfaces and arrives at the receiver from many different directions. Since the sound power level of each source contributes to both the direct and reverberant sound, the most effective noise mitigation approach is to minimize the sound power of the sources themselves. As a secondary measure, the reverberant sound field can be reduced through the use of generous amounts of suitably selected sound-absorbing materials on the room surfaces.

9.8 LIMITS ON THE SOUND PRESSURE LEVELS IN DATACOM FACILITIES

Various regulatory agencies in the industrialized countries have established acoustical noise exposure limits in the workplace to protect employees against permanent hearing loss. As examples, in the United States, the regulatory agency is the Occupational Safety and Health Administration (OSHA) and in Europe, it is the European Union (EU). The regulations vary in their specific limits, with the European occupational noise limits being a bit more stringent than OSHA's. As a general statement, however, the A-weighted sound pressure levels averaged over an eight-hour period should not exceed 90 dB(A) under the OSHA regulations or 87 dB(A) under the EU regulations under any circumstances. Lower levels, such as 80 dB(A) and 85 dB(A), are defined to trigger certain mandatory actions by the employer or owner, including initiating hearing conservation and monitoring programs or making hearing protection freely available to employees. Although these levels are relatively high and aimed more at protecting factory and manufacturing area workers, densely populated data centers may still run the risk of exceeding the OSHA or EU noise limits and potentially causing hearing damage. To be safe and certain, datacom managers and planners should consult the appropriate OSHA regulations and guidelines (USDOL 1991) and the EU Directives (EU 2003) or enlist the services of a qualified acoustical consultant or industrial hygienist.

The noise levels in smaller, more typical data centers are not usually high enough to cause hearing damage but should be controlled to avoid employee or customer complaints due to annoyance, difficulty concentrating, interference with communication, or other nonauditory effects of the noise. To protect against these effects, many guidelines have been published over the years by various agencies and organizations, specifying maximum sound pressure levels for different environments. For commercial business areas, which might include datacom centers, the consensus is that the average sound pressure levels should not exceed 70 dB(A) where personnel are located. The World Health Organization (WHO) Guidelines (Berglund 1999) recommend this level but in a note state that the goal is also to prevent hearing damage. To put this level in perspective, the WHO guideline (to avoid annoyance) for classrooms and homes is $L_{pA} = 35$ dB(A) and for general outdoor residential areas, $L_{pA} = 55$ dB(A). The emission sound power level limits, mentioned above, defined for generally attended data centers, were derived, in fact, to allow data centers with typical equipment layout densities to meet this $L_{pA} = 70$ dB(A) specification.

10

Structural and Seismic

Datacom equipment such as high-performance computers and servers, storage servers, networking equipment, and rack-mounted equipment, can impose considerable load to the building, floor structure, and floor covering panels. The effect of the datacom equipment on the building floor and floor panels will be discussed in the following sections.

10.1   BUILDING FLOOR STRUCTURE

10.1.1   Weight Distribution Area

The weight distribution area consists of the equipment or machine area and some part of the service clearance area.

The machine area is the area directly beneath the equipment defined by the length and width dimensions representing the equipment's perimeter. This machine area is represented as A in the formulas in the next section.

The service clearance area is the area around the machine. Service clearance areas of adjacent machines may overlap. The size of the service clearances depends on the application of the equipment and the expected environment in which the equipment will be installed. When the machine is installed against a wall, the service clearance area should permit front-end servicing or adequate provisions should be made to facilitate movement as required.

The weight distribution area is the area around the machine and it is represented as S in the formulas in next section. Weight distribution areas may not overlap. Given that service clearance areas can overlap but weight distribution areas cannot, when two pieces of equipment are installed next to one another, only half the area between the equipment can be used for weight distribution for either machine. If the result is not sufficient for proper weight distribution, the distance x between the machines has to be increased until the proper distribution is achieved.

10.1.2 Floor Loading/Floor Load Rating

A subfloor or building floor maximum allowable distributed load varies from building to building. Some datacom equipment facilities are constructed with floors rated to support a uniformly distributed load of 70 lb/ft^2 (3450 N/m^2). In any case, it is important to verify the allowable floor loading capacity. In order to estimate the uniform distributed load, it is necessary to define the component of the loads imparted by the datacom equipment and the related activities or equipment involved in datacom equipment installation, such as the live load and the system cable loads.

The live load is the weight imposed around the equipment in the weight distribution area by personnel traffic, test equipment, and various carts and documentation. This live load represented as $K1$ is estimated to be 15 lb/ft^2 (750 N/m^2) for the examples in the next section.

In many cases, datacom equipment is installed in a raised-floor environment, which is a structure used to create a floor area above the building structural floor to facilitate cabling and chilled-air distribution. The raised floor and the system cables impose a distributed load estimated to be 10 lb/ft^2 (500 N/m^2). This factor is represented as $K2$ in the examples in the next section

Both $K1$ and $K2$ factors can be adjusted upward. For example, high-performance communication equipment with heavy cables may need to have higher $K2$ values.

10.1.3 Floor Loading Calculation General Formulas

The weight of the equipment to be installed must be such that the floor loading (FL) will be less than or equal to the building floor load rating (FLR).

The floor loading (FL) is equal to:

$$FL = \frac{M + (K1 \times S) + K2(S + A)}{S + A} \tag{10.1}$$

where

FLR = maximum floor load rating in N/ m^2

FL = floor loading in N/m^2

M = datacom equipment weight in N

$K1$ = live load in the weight distribution area at 15 lb/ft^2

$K2$ = raised floor/cable load for the area at 10 lb/ft^2

A = machine area in m^2

S = weight distribution area in m^2

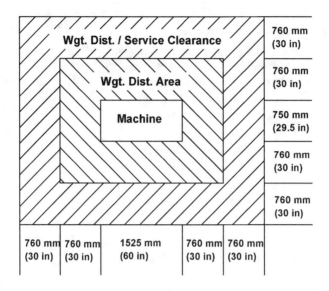

Figure 10.1 Weight distribution area. Reproduced with permission from IBM (2001).

10.1.4 Floor Loading Calculation Examples

Example 1. Given a frame weighing 1124 lb (5000 N) with a footprint of 29.5 × 60 in. (750 × 1525 mm) and a weight distribution area as shown in Figure 10.1, the machine floor loading (*FL*) is determined as follows:

$$A = 0.75 \times 1.525 = 1.144 \text{ m}^2$$

$$S + A = (0.75 + 0.76 + 0.76) \times (1.525 + 0.76 + 0.76) = 6.912 \text{ m}^2$$

$$S = 6.912 \text{ m}^2 - 1.144 \text{ m}^2 = 5.768 \text{ m}^2$$

$$FL = 5000 + (750 \times 5.768) + (500 \times 6.912) / (6.912) = 1849.2 \text{ N/ m}^2 \text{ (38.6 lb/ft}^2)$$

Example 2. A multiple-frame machine configuration is to be installed as a group (four frames total).

Machine dimensions: 0.75 m × 1 m
Machine weight: 1348 lb (6000 N)
Service clearance:
    Front and rear: 1.2 m
    Between frames: 0 m
    Left and right of group of frames: 1 m

Use half the service clearance dimensions ($1.2/2 = 0.6$ m and $1/2 = 0.5$ m) for calculating the weight distribution area.

Check to see if the weight distribution area based solely on the service clearance will result in FL = 70 lb/ft^2 (3450 N/m^2) or less. (Half of the service clearance area distance is used assuming additional groups of frames could be placed with only the service clearance between them and this group.)

First check the four-frame system as a whole:

$$M = 6000 \times 4 = 24{,}000 \text{ N}$$

$$A = (0.75 \times 1) \times 4 = 3 \text{ m}^2$$

$$S = \{(1 \text{ m}/2 \times 2) + 0.75 \text{ m} \times 4\} \times (1.2/2 \text{ m} + 1 \text{ m} + 1.2/2 \text{ m}) - A = 5.8 \text{ m}^2$$

$$S + A = 5.8 \text{ m}^2 + 3 \text{ m}^2 = 8.8 \text{ m}^2$$

$$FL = 24{,}000 + (750 \times 5.8) + (500 \times 8.8)/(8.8) = 3721 \text{ N/m}^2 \ (78.15 \text{ lb/ft}^2)$$

In this example, assuming the allowable uniformly distributed floor loading is 70 lb/ft^2 (3450 N/m^2), the service clearance area must be increased in order to increase the weight distribution area.

10.2   ACCESS FLOOR PANELS AND STRUCTURE

Access floor panel manufacturers specify different loading limits. Four limits are critical for datacom equipment installation. They are the concentrated load, uniform load, ultimate load, and rolling load (Maxcess 2005; Tate 2005).

Most installations of datacom equipment will need holes in floor panels for cable routings and other purposes. Depending on the size and location of the floor panel holes, the allowable load limits will be lower than the limits listed by the panel floor manufacturer. The lower limit values can be as much as 50% of the specified limits. This is not a cause for concern in areas limited to pedestrian traffic or furniture loads. Where a panel with a hole may be subject to equipment loads or rolling loads, it is standard practice to permanently support it with two additional support pedestals at opposite sides of the cutout. Panels with round grommet holes 5 in. (127 mm) in diameter or less need no additional support.

10.2.1   Concentrated Load

The concentrated load capacity of a floor panel is defined as the capability of the access floor panel to withstand a load placed on a one-square-inch area with a resulting deflection no more than 0.100 in. (2.54 mm) and a permanent set no more than 0.010 in. (0.254 mm) when the load is removed. The concentrated load capacity of an access floor panel varies from 1000 lb (4445 N) to 3,500 lb (15,572 N) depending on the type and manufacturer of the floor panel. *Note*: The term *concentrated load* is synonymous with the term *point load* where used in access floor loading criteria.

For a multiple-equipment machine configuration to be installed as a group, one floor panel can be subjected to two point loads. One of the casters from each adjacent machine can impart a high load on a panel floor. For a machine weighing M, the nominal caster load is $M/3$ and the worst case in $M/2$. At a given time only three of the four casters (a plane is defined by three points) will bear the total weight of the equipment. For equipment that is heavy on one side, resulting in load concentration, the worst case value of $M/2$ should be used.

10.2.2   Uniform Load

The uniform load capacity of an access floor panel is defined as the panel's square-foot load capacity and is 25% of the panel's concentrated load capacity. Top surface deflection resulting from uniform loading will be no more than 0.060 in. (1.52 mm) and permanent set no more than 0.010 in. (0.254 mm) after the load is removed. The uniform load imparted by equipment weighing M and with the machine area equal to A is equal to M/A.

10.2.3   Ultimate Load

The ultimate load capacity of an access floor panel is defined as the maximum load the access floor panel can withstand without failing when a load is applied on a 1 in.^{2} (645 mm^2) area of the panel.

The concentrated load imparted by equipment is similar to the concentrated load discussed above.

10.2.4   Rolling Load

The rolling load is defined as the capability of an access floor panel to withstand a rolling load of specific wheel diameter and width and imparting a deformation no greater than 0.040 in. (1 mm). For a piece of equipment weighing M, the nominal rolling load per caster is $M/3$ and the worst case is $M/2$. Rolling load capability is designated for infrequent heavy equipment loads (based on a 10-pass test) and for frequent non-equipment loads (based on a 10,000-pass test).

10.2.5   Stringer vs. Stringerless Understructure Systems

Stringer systems are used where additional lateral pedestal stability is required to resist heavy rolling loads or seismic loads. Stringers are used extensively in computer rooms and telecom switch rooms due to rolling loads imposed by equipment movement and in heavy load areas such as service corridors, print rooms, and light industrial facilities. Additionally, the use of gravity-held floor panels in lieu of cornerlock (bolt-down) panels in the system allows fast access to the underfloor cavity. Stringer systems are typically used in conjunction with floor panels that have permanently bonded floor tiles. Finished floor heights generally range from 6 in. (152 mm) to 60 in. (1524 mm).

Stringerless systems (also referred to as bolt-down or cornerlock) are used in general office areas and in pedestrian traffic areas, such as corridors, classrooms, call centers, and retail spaces. The floor panels for a stringerless system are typically supplied without a permanently bonded floor covering for application of removable field-applied carpet tiles. Finished floor heights range from 3 in. (76 mm) to 24 in. (609 mm).

10.2.6 Floor Panel Load Ratings

Manufacturers provide floor panels in several concentrated load ratings ranging from 1000 lb (4445 N) to 3,500 lb (15,572 N) to accommodate a variety of loading requirements at minimal cost. Panels with load ratings of 1000 lb (4445 N) or 1250 lb (5560 N) are typically utilized for office floors, computer rooms, and pedestrian traffic areas. Panels with load ratings of 1500 lb (6672 N) to 2500 lb (11,120 N) are used for heavy static load and/or rolling load requirements such as those of service corridors, casinos, and printing or light industrial facilities. Panels with load ratings of 3,500 lb (15,572 N), or greater, are used in heavy industrial areas and in tool or equipment moving paths.

10.2.7 Access Floors in Seismic Areas

Access floor systems can be installed in seismic regions by the use of seismic-grade floor pedestals, which may be attached to the subfloor either by adhesive or by expansion anchors into the concrete, depending upon calculated seismic loads. Some projects may require bracing of some percentage of the pedestals due to heavy floor loading or high floor conditions or a combination of severe conditions. Four-foot-long stringers are utilized extensively for floors in high seismic regions due to the lateral resistance added by the horizontal members fixed at the top of the pedestal system. For projects in seismic regions, the determination of understructure system requirements are based on lateral force calculations in accordance with applicable building codes.

10.3 DATACOM EQUIPMENT INSTALLATION IN AN EARTHQUAKE AREA

In earthquake areas, to ensure personnel safety and to reduce datacom equipment damage, different types of earthquake-resistant installation methods are available (Maxcess 2005; Notohardjono 2003). In certain areas it may be required to rigidly tie down the equipment to the building subfloor. In this case, for a raised-floor installation, the floor panels need to have attachment holes at each corner of the equipment. When designing a system for seismic resistance, not only the structural integrity should be considered, but also the continuous operation, as well as preventing the frame from toppling over. Specifically, critical computer equipment must also remain operational during earthquake events, and the datacom equipment should not induce any safety hazard to the occupants, namely, no flying hardware that potentially can injure occupants.

In general, the earthquake-resistant design goal is to have the datacom equipment structure, floor panels, and structure able to resist 1 G horizontal forces and any overturning moments resulting from application of the 1 G force at the base of the equipment. A test performed on equipment weighing 3372 lb (15,000 N) showed that the vertical compression force between the equipment base and the subfloor (for an 18 in. raised floor) can be as high as 21,244 lb (94,500 N). Consequently, the floor panel and its structure should be able to withstand that amount of vertical compression force.

A system designed to withstand an earthquake includes the design of the tie-down system, the frame structure, and the mounting of the subassemblies to their support frame. The tie-down hardware is used to rigidly secure the frame structures to the floor, ensuring that the system will not tip over while reducing the amount of displacement, especially in the horizontal direction. A typical tie-down the turn-buckle system is shown in Figures 10.2 and 10.3. This type of tie-down has been proven to perform satisfactorily for a system weighing up to 3709 lb (16,500 N). In addition, the turnbuckle system also induces a high initial compressive load between the building subfloor and the datacom equipment, which prevents relative movement between the equipment and the floor panel and building subfloor.

Generally, the datacom equipment structure inherently can withstand the vertical vibration better than the horizontal vibration. The narrow width of the datacom equipment is the primary concern for seismic motions.

An additional seismic design that is neither invasive nor floor-access limiting is the overhead snubbing technique as shown in Figure 10-4.

To have an earthquake-resistant datacom center, there are several choices of raised-floor panel structures, tie-down methods, and, lastly, of course, datacom equipment itself. The choice of the tie-down method depends on the availability of data to support the actual configuration of datacom equipment to be installed and the ease of installation. An actual test with the authentic tie-down brackets used to stiffen the equipment and the actual datacom equipment itself is highly recommended to ensure the whole system is behaving as expected. It should be noted that in certain areas, the local ordinances or building codes may require a rigid tie-down connection between the equipment and building subfloor.

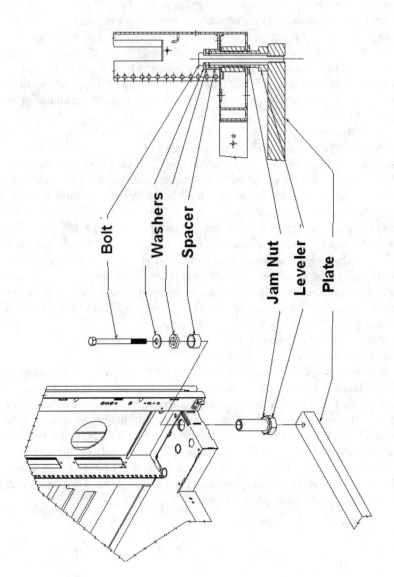

Bolt

Washers

Spacer

Jam Nut

Leveler

Plate

Figure 10.2 Rigid tie-down—turnbuckle assembly. Reproduced with permission from Notohardjono (2004).

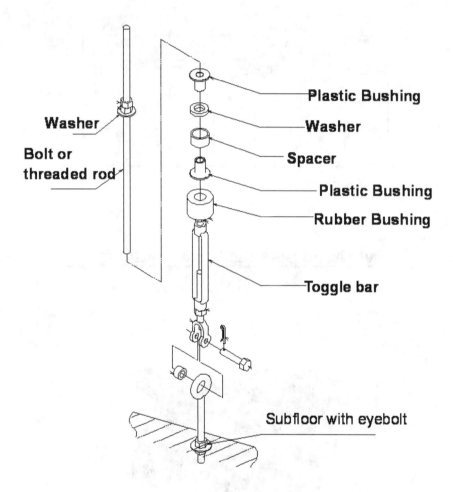

Figure 10.3 Rigid tie-down—detail turnbuckle assembly. Reproduced with permission from Notohardjono (2003).

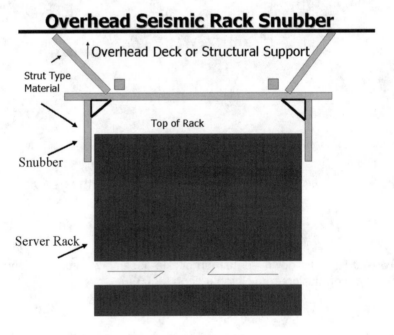

Figure 10.4 Overhead seismic rack snubber.

11

Fire Detection and Suppression

The design of the fire suppression system for a high-reliability environment must go beyond basic life safety. The system's objectives are to protect personnel, equipment, and structure and to minimize or eliminate downtime. Suppression designs may go well beyond code requirements (typically National Fire Protection Association [NFPA] standards) in order to meet these objectives. Code compliance and overall scope of the system design must be at the forefront.

Using a holistic approach, the complexity of the system design should correlate with the overall project objectives. Selection of the components, extinguishing media, zoning, and sequence of operations must complement the project as a whole and must address the degree of protection that the client has established.

Important design considerations include (1) detection of fire at its incipient stage, (2) application of effective automatic means to suppress the incipient fire, and (3) early notification to personnel allowing early intervention.

11.1   FIRE ALARM SYSTEMS

The fire alarm system is the first line of defense in the high-reliability environment. An intelligent, addressable system is best suited for application in these rapidly changing environments because of its functional flexibility and capacity for future expansion.

11.1.1   Fire Detection Methodologies: Types of Detectors and Applications

11.1.1.1 Smoke-Sensing Fire Detectors

One of the best ways of proactively monitoring for a fire condition is to sense for smoke. Typically, smoke in some form will be present well in advance of sufficient heat to activate a detector. Considering that the detection of smoke relies on smoke entering the detection chamber or passing the detection elements, many considerations must be taken into account when spacing detection, whether using the NFPA 72 prescriptive method or performance method.

- In high-airflow environments, when following the prescriptive method of spacing detectors, spot-type smoke detectors must have their spacing reduced based on the table/graph given in NFPA 72-2002 associated with paragraph 5.7.5.3. In all cases the manufacturer's documented instructions should be followed, especially with regard to air velocity ratings.
- In many data centers, to accomplish the wide spans of open area, deep structural beams on the ceiling are present. The selection of detector locations within these beam pockets should be carefully made. For ceiling heights exceeding 12 ft and beam depths exceeding 12 in., the beam is essentially equivalent to a full-height partition with regard to detector spacing. Refer to NFPA 72-2002, paragraph 5.7.3.2.4, for further information.

In a photoelectric light-scattering smoke detector, a light source and a photosensitive sensor are arranged so the rays from the light source do not normally fall on the photosensitive sensor. When smoke particles enter the light path, some of the light is scattered by reflection and refraction onto the sensor, causing the detector to respond. In a photoelectric obscuration-type smoke detector, a light source is transmitted directly to a receiving photosensitive device. When smoke particles enter the light path, light is obscured from the photosensitive device, causing the detector to respond.

Light-scattering-type detectors do not respond well to dark-colored smoke because the dark materials absorb light and reduce scattering.

An ionization smoke detector contains a small amount of radioactive material that ionizes the air in the sensing chamber, making the air conductive and permitting current to flow between two charged electrodes. This gives the sensing chamber an effective electrical conductance. When smoke particles enter the ionization area, they decrease the conductance of the air by attaching themselves to the ions, causing a reduction in mobility. When the conductance is less than a predetermined level, the detector responds with an alarm.

Since smoke detection is accomplished by ionizing the air in the chamber, this method of detection does not perform well in a high-airflow environment.

A duct smoke detector is a device or group of devices used to detect the presence of smoke in the airstream of ductwork sections of the HVAC air-handling systems. Typical smoke detection devices used for duct application include smoke detector sensors within a housing mounted outside the duct utilizing sampling tubes, area smoke detectors listed for in-duct or partial in-duct mounting, a light beam detector consisting of projector and receiver mounted within the duct and an air sampling type detector.

An air-sampling detector consists of a piping or tubing distribution network that runs from the detector to the area(s) to be protected. An aspiration fan in the detector housing draws air from the protected area back to the detector through air-sampling ports, piping, or tubing. At the detector, the air is analyzed for fire products.

Laser-based air sampling uses the principle of photoelectric detection to monitor the air in the detection chamber.

Cloud chamber-based air sampling takes a sample of air from the protected area into a high-humidity chamber with the detector. After the air sample has been raised to a high humidity, the pressure is lowered slightly. If smoke particles are present, the moisture in the air condenses on them, forming a cloud in the chamber. The density of this cloud is then measured by a photoelectric principle. The detector responds when the density is greater than a predetermined level.

A projected beam smoke detector is a type of photoelectric light-obscuration smoke detector wherein the beam spans the protected area. This type of detector utilizes a transmitter on one end and a receiver on the other and may be used when mounted close to a surface that will reflect the beam (suspended ceiling). A reflected beam type uses a transmitter/receiver on one end and a mirror on the other. These offer wide-ranging areas of protection.

11.1.1.2 Heat-Sensing Fire Detectors

A spot-type fixed-temperature detector is a device that detects abnormally high temperature. It is available in several settings, 135°F (57°C) and higher.

A spot-type rate-compensated detector is a device that responds when the temperature of the air surrounding the device reaches a predetermined level, regardless of the rate of temperature rise.

A spot-type rate-of-rise detector is a device that responds when the temperature rises at a rate exceeding a predetermined value.

A line-type detector is a device in which detection is continuous along a path. Typical examples are rate-of-rise pneumatic tubing detectors and heat-sensitive cable.

11.1.1.3 Radiant-Energy-Sensing Fire Detectors

Infrared (IR) detectors respond to flaming fires emitting light in the infrared portion of the spectrum. These detectors are designed to alarm to hydrocarbon fires while ignoring things such as arc welding, nuclear radiation, and x-rays. IR detectors are available in single wavelength or dual wavelength.

Ultraviolet (UV) detectors respond to flaming fires emitting light in the ultraviolet portion of the spectrum. These detectors should not be used around arc welding, as they will respond to the ultraviolet light given off by the welding process.

Ultraviolet-infrared (UV-IR) detectors respond to flaming fires emitting light in both the ultraviolet and infrared portion of the light spectrum. UV-IR detectors require both the UV and the IR sensors to alarm simultaneously. This makes them very resistant to false alarms (e.g., from welding, x-rays, lightning, artificial lighting, and interrupted hot body radiation) because while there are sources in the environment other than fire that will cause the UV sensor or the IR sensor to false alarm, the sensors have virtually none of these sources in common.

11.1.1.4 Suppression-Related Conditions

Sprinkler water flow alarm: A switch mounted to a sprinkler or standpipe pipe is remotely monitored by the fire alarm control panel. Water flow produces a change in the switch's internal contact position, initiating a fire alarm. Alarm delay is possible to avoid false alarms due to water hammer condition.

Control valve tamper supervisory: A switch mounted to a sprinkler or standpipe valve is monitored by the remote fire alarm control panel. Motion of the valve handle from the normally open position produces a change in the switch's internal contact position, initiating a trouble alarm.

Low-pressure supervisory: A switch mounted to a sprinkler or standpipe pipe, typically for a pre-action sprinkler system. If activated, it produces a change in its internal contact position for remote monitoring by the fire alarm control panel.

Suppression abort: A control button, typically located at the egress doors or the releasing control panel, to manually delay release of a suppression agent. When the button is released, the releasing sequence resumes.

Fire Pump running, phase reversal, and power failure: These conditions are monitored by the fire pump controller and reported to the remote fire alarm control panel as fire alarm (pump running) or trouble signals (phase reversal, power failure).

Clean agent system release: If initiated by a separate releasing panel, this action causes a change in the releasing panel's internal contact position, initiating an alarm at the remote fire alarm control panel. Alternatively, the releasing function can be performed by the remote fire alarm control panel.

11.1.2 Applications of Smoke/Fire Detection Systems

11.1.2.1 Life Safety Detection and Alarm

Control, monitoring, and detection devices and equipment are typically required to be listed and approved for the environment in which they are installed. An analog addressable fire alarm system with capacity suitable for future modifications should be provided. Primary and secondary power sources are required.

Some building codes identify data centers as use group "B" and may not require automatic detection in most areas of the facility. In addition, building codes may not require manual alarm activation. Although automatic detection and manual activation may not be required throughout the facility, complete coverage, as defined in NFPA 72, should be provided to mitigate a smoke/fire condition and prevent spread to other areas of the facility.

11.1.2.2 Critical Spaces—Above the Floor

Photoelectric-type spot smoke detectors and/or air-sampling-type smoke detectors should be provided to monitor smoke conditions near the ceiling. In most cases this will be either the underside of the suspended ceiling or underside of the structural ceiling slab, whichever is lower. Where combustibles will be present above a suspended ceiling, and the structural ceiling slab is accessible, detection may be provided to offer additional sensing coverage. Where optional fire suppression is installed above a suspended ceiling, detection will be required for activation

Where an air-sampling system is installed as one of two types of protection monitoring a common horizontal surface (underside of the suspended ceiling or underside of the structural ceiling slab), the air-sampling detection should be connected as supplemental and monitored by the fire alarm system for supervisory conditions only and not activate alarm, fire suppression activation, fan shutdown, or evacuation.

Although NFPA 72 and NFPA 90A permit the use of area detection to perform required HVAC equipment shutdowns, the use of duct detectors for this purpose is greatly preferred.

Where smoke detection is provided, it can be programmed to activate fire suppression systems. Where additional reliability is desired, spot-type combination heat detectors may be provided to activate the fire suppression system, leaving the smoke detection for evacuation. Where multiple fire suppression systems are provided, smoke detection can be used to activate the alarm and clean agent fire suppression system, and the heat detection would activate the water-based system.

11.1.2.3 Critical Spaces—Below the Floor

Provide photoelectric-type spot smoke detectors and/or air-sampling-type smoke detectors to monitor smoke conditions on the underside of the raised floor tiles. Where optional fire suppression is to be installed below the raised floor, detection must be provided for activation.

Where the jurisdiction follows the 2002 version (or later) of the National Electric Code (NEC), and the choice to utilize the leniencies provided by Article 645 of the NEC is selected and air is transported below the floor, detection of smoke below the floor must cause air circulation below the floor to cease. Many jurisdictions will allow this event to occur upon activation of a second device (cross zoning) and/or alarm verification. One of the leniencies provided by Article 645 includes certain types of non-plenum rated cables to be placed below the raised floor.

To reduce congestion of devices and other equipment below the floor, install smoke detectors and/or air-sampling pipes on the raised-floor pedestals, as close to the underside of the raised-floor tiles as possible.

11.1.2.4 Support Services Spaces Critical to Environment Maintenance

Provide photoelectric-type spot smoke detectors and/or air-sampling-type smoke detectors to monitor smoke conditions near the ceiling. In most cases this will be either the underside of the suspended ceiling or underside of the structural ceiling slab, whichever is lower. Where combustibles will be present above a suspended ceiling, and the structural ceiling slab is accessible, detection may be provided to offer additional sensing coverage. Where optional fire suppression is installed above a suspended ceiling, provide detection for activation.

Provide duct detection for supply and return airflow, and shut down the associated fan system only upon alarm.

Where computer room air-conditioning units/handlers are used, provide photoelectric spot-type smoke detectors and/or air-sampling-type smoke detectors in the return air path. Use the spot-type smoke detectors to shut down the associated fan system only upon alarm. Where air-sampling detection is provided as a supplementary smoke detection system, it should not activate fan shutdown.

11.1.2.5 Support Services Spaces Critical to Power Supply

See 11.1.2.2, "Critical Spaces—Above the Floor."

11.1.2.6 Noncritical Support Services Spaces

Provide photoelectric-type spot smoke detectors to monitor smoke conditions near the ceiling. In most cases this will be either the underside of the suspended ceiling or underside of the structural ceiling slab, whichever is lower. Where combustibles will be present above a suspended ceiling, and the structural ceiling slab is accessible, detection may be provided to offer additional sensing coverage. Where fire suppression is provided above a suspended ceiling, provide detection as required for activation.

11.1.3 Basic Functions

11.1.3.1 Life Safety Detection and Alarm

The general category of fire alarm circuits is divided into two types: initiating device circuits and notification device circuits. Different configurations of these circuits can be categorized as Class A and Class B. Class A circuits communicate through two communication paths (ring-type circuit) and Class B circuits use one (radial-type circuit). Class A circuits are not required by code, but their installation may reduce system downtime (and thus increase facility protection) during repair cycles.

11.1.3.2 Suppression System Monitoring

Where a building fire alarm system is listed as a releasing panel, it may actuate a suppression system directly. A separate releasing panel may be used, but detection must be directly connected to it to make it a complete system. Some approvals, such as Factory Mutual, require particular releasing modules with certain valves, solenoids, etc. A system is required to be monitored for trouble, alarm, and supervisory conditions.

11.1.3.3 Suppression System Actuation and Release

Pre-action systems can be single interlock or double interlock, monitored and released by a building or dedicated fire alarm system. Dedicated fire alarm systems for releasing must be monitored by the building fire alarm system.

11.1.3.4 Interface with Mechanical Systems

Interface between the fire alarm system and mechanical systems includes both required and non-required actions. Where interruption of airflow is required, fans should be shut down by interruption of the fan motor controller. This can be accomplished by the use of a monitored control module in the fire alarm panel or directly through an electrical contact in the detector. Motorized smoke or combination fire/smoke dampers are required to be controlled from the fire alarm panel. Elevator recall is similarly required to be controlled from the fire alarm panel. The closing of required fire doors throughout the building is also required to be initiated by the fire alarm control panel.

11.1.4 Notification Devices

11.1.4.1 Audible

In most cases, horn-type audible notification devices are acceptable. Where required by local codes or where the layout of the facility could benefit from a voice-type system, speakers can be used to provide notification of events. Both horns and speakers, when used, are required to be audible to standards set forth in the fire alarm code.

11.1.4.2 Visual

Strobe-type visual devices are typically required by code to be provided throughout the facility, specifically in nonprivate rooms such as the data center, corridors, bathrooms, infrastructure rooms, lobbies, etc. Where multiple strobes are visible from any single position on the floor, the strobes are required to be synchronized to reduce the net flashing effects on the person in the room.

11.1.4.3 Annunciators

Annunciators can be either graphic or alphanumeric with interface to Command Center computer workstations if desired.

11.1.4.4 Printer

Printers are optional devices useful for providing automatic text records of system activity. They can also print graphic representations of the Fire Command Center workstation output.

11.1.5 Manually Actuated Pull Station

Manual alarm devices (pull stations) are required to be located in accordance with the applicable building code and are recommended in all major support rooms to provide an opportunity for manual early warning.

11.1.6 Identification

Particular attention should be paid to identification of device addresses, circuit identification, and connection diagrams.

11.1.7 System Documentation

Operation and maintenance (O&M) manuals and as-built drawings must be maintained for maintenance and troubleshooting.

11.1.8 Inspection, Testing, and Maintenance

NFPA 72 requires periodic maintenance for all devices.

11.2 FIRE SUPPRESSION SYSTEMS

Once detected, fire suppression systems are used to extinguish and mitigate the potentially destructive effects of fire. A number of agents are available to accomplish this, each with specific advantages applicable to a particular circumstance.

Fire suppression systems for high-reliability environments fall into two general categories: those using water and those using clean agents.

11.2.1 Clean Agent Systems

Clean agent systems combat fire by reducing the oxygen content of the space, absorbing the heat of the fire, interfering with the chemistry of combustion, or a combination of these activities. Usually, they rely on a fire detection and alarm system for actuation, although small-volume systems of some agents have been developed that are self-actuating. Smoke or fire detectors sense the presence of fire in the protected facility. The detection and control panel then sounds an alarm, shuts down air handlers (if so programmed), disconnects power from the protected equipment (if so programmed), and releases agent into the protected area.

11.2.1.1 Carbon Dioxide

Carbon dioxide (CO_2) offers a number of advantages compared to other non-water-based agents.

- When properly designed, engineered, and installed, CO_2 fire suppression systems will not normally damage electronic equipment.
- CO_2 leaves no residual associated with its use as a fire-suppressing agent.
- When properly ventilated, the gas escapes to the atmosphere after the fire has been extinguished.

Carbon dioxide gas has a high ratio of expansion, facilitating rapid discharge and allowing for three-dimensional penetration of the entire hazard area quickly. CO_2 extinguishes a fire by reducing the oxygen content of the protected area below the point where it can support combustion. Due to its extreme density, CO_2 quickly and effectively permeates the protected hazard area and suppresses the fire. Rapid expansion of the CO_2 gas reduces the ambient temperature in the protected hazard area, aiding in the extinguishing process and retarding reignition.

CO_2 fire extinguishing systems typically store the agent in one of two different ways: in high-pressure cylinders or in low-pressure CO_2 tanks.

CO_2 fire extinguishing agent is comparatively inexpensive and readily available. The major drawback to CO_2 is its unsuitability for use in occupied spaces due to the reduction in oxygen content that it causes.

11.2.1.2 FM-200 or HFC-227

HFC-227 or FM-200, chemically known as heptafluoropropane, is an alternative fire suppression system agent manufactured in the United States by Great Lakes Chemical (FM-200) and DuPont Corporation (HFC-227). It is a replacement for the ozone-depleting halon 1301 used extensively before 1994. General properties are as follows:

- There is no ozone depletion potential (its ODP is zero).
- It is safe for use when people are present. Toxicology studies show that people can be exposed to normal extinguishing concentrations without suffering residual health problems.
- Similar to CO_2, FM-200 fire suppression systems will not damage sensitive electronic equipment.
- It leaves no residue.
- When properly ventilated, the gas escapes to the atmosphere after the fire has been extinguished.

The extinguishing agent is typically stored in cylinders or spheres and is delivered to distribution nozzles through a system piping network.

11.2.1.3 Novec 1230

Novec 1230 (manufactured by Ansul Corporation) is an environmentally benign halon replacement alternative to HFCs. It can be used in occupied areas. Novec 1230 fluid can effectively be applied in streaming, flooding, inerting, and explosion suppression applications.

11.2.1.4 Ecaro-25

ECARO-25, or FE-25, is a clean agent fire-extinguishing chemical developed by the Dupont Co.

Like FM-200, it is a recognized alternative to halon 1301.

Ecaro-25 provides an effective drop-in replacement to halon. This agent can work in existing halon piping networks, requiring only replacement of the nozzles and containers to transform a halon 1301 system to an Ecaro-25 system.

General properties of ECARO-25 are:

- It is noncorrosive.
- It is electrically nonconductive.
- It leaves no residue.
- It is suited for fire protection in normally occupied spaces, appearing to display no adverse toxicological effects.

11.2.1.5 Inergen Extinguishing Systems

Inergen extinguishing systems are designed for total flooding protection against Class A surface burning, Class B flammable liquid, and Class C fires occurring within an enclosure. The action of Inergen is to lower the oxygen content of the space below the level that supports combustion. Engineered by Ansul Corporation, it is a mixture of three naturally occurring gases: nitrogen (52%), argon (40%), and carbon dioxide (8%). It is suitable for hazards where an electrical, nonconductive medium is essential or desirable; where cleanup of other agents presents a problem; where hazard obstructions require the use of a gaseous agent; or where the hazard is normally occupied and requires a nontoxic agent.

Inergen is derived from naturally occurring gases present in the earth's atmosphere. It exhibits no ozone-depleting potential, does not contribute to global warming, nor does it contribute unique chemical species with extended atmospheric lifetimes. Because of its composition, it does not exhibit the toxicity drawbacks associated with the chemically derived agents.

When the Inergen agent is discharged into a room, it extinguishes fire by lowering the oxygen content below the level required to support combustion, while still allowing people to breathe in the reduced-oxygen atmosphere. It reduces the oxygen content of a space from its normal 21% to approximately 12.5% (when the oxygen content is reduced below 15%, most ordinary combustibles will not burn.), while increasing the carbon dioxide content from 1% (normal) to about 4%. This stimulates the human body to breathe more deeply and rapidly to compensate for the lower oxygen content of the atmosphere.

Inergen is an effective fire-extinguishing agent that can be used on many types of fires. Inergen extinguishing system units are designed for total flooding protection against Class A surface burning, Class B flammable liquid, and Class C fires occurring within an enclosure by lowering the oxygen content below the level that supports combustion.

11.2.2 Water-Based Systems

All fire sprinkler systems are water based; they are differentiated in the passive (nondischarge) system condition: wet system piping is filled with water or water-based solutions; dry systems have water introduced through a number of means.

11.2.2.1 Wet Pipe Sprinkler System

Wet pipe sprinkler systems are the most common and most reliable type of sprinkler protection. The entire piping network is filled with water under pressure in all wet pipe sprinkler systems. Upon the operation of a fusible link or other type of thermal element, water is discharged over the protected hazard.

Since there are no delays in sprinkler system operation, wet sprinkler systems are preferred by authorities having jurisdiction. Wet sprinkler systems are the most economically sound. Wet sprinkler systems are limited by code and NFPA 13 to 52,000 ft^2 (4830 m^2) area per system.

11.2.2.2 Dry Pipe Sprinkler System

Dry pipe sprinkler systems are usually provided in unheated buildings and/or in areas that may be exposed to freezing temperatures. The piping network in the dry pipe systems is filled with supervised pressurized air or nitrogen gas. Similar to wet pipe system components, fusible link type sprinkler heads are used. The operation of a sprinkler head causes an air pressure drop in the system, opening a clapper on a dry pipe valve and allowing water to flow through the system and discharge through any open sprinkler heads.

Dry pipe systems are more complex than wet pipe systems and cause a delay in water discharge over the hazard. Code-compliant dry pipe systems do not exceed 750 gallons (3410 liters) capacity and must deliver water to the most remote sprinkler head within 60 seconds.

11.2.2.3 Deluge Sprinkler System

Deluge sprinkler systems are required where the hazard is substantial and great amounts of water are required to control a fire and/or to separate two fire hazards. A typical installation would be protection inside a fuel storage tank room.

A deluge system contains open sprinkler nozzles connected to a nonpressurized piping system. Deluge systems are controlled by a deluge valve, which is monitored by a detection system. Operation of a detection device will open the deluge valve and allow water flow through all sprinkler nozzles simultaneously.

11.2.2.4 Pre-Action Sprinkler System

Pre-action systems are more complex than wet and dry pipe systems as they contain more components and equipment. Pre-action systems require specialized knowledge and experience in design and installation, and the inspection, testing and maintenance activities needed to ensure their reliability and functionality are more involved.

Pre-action sprinkler systems require a detection system covering the protected area for operation.

There are three basic types of pre-action systems, which are identified by their mode of operation: non-interlock, single interlock, and double interlock. Additional variations, such as the use of a cross-zoned smoke detection system, are possible.

A non-interlocked system admits water to the sprinkler piping upon the operation of detection device or when a sprinkler activates.

A single-interlocked system admits water to the sprinkler piping upon the operation of a detection device. Opening of a sprinkler head will only cause a trouble alarm (due to the drop in supervising air pressure).

A double-interlocked system admits water to the sprinkler piping only upon the operation of both a detection device (initiating a fire alarm and opening the valve) and a fusible sprinkler element (to release the air pressure in the pipe). Only activation of a detector will initiate a fire alarm; Only opening of a sprinkler will initiate a trouble alarm.

11.2.2.5 Fire Cycle

This system provides a water-based fire suppression system with an automatic shutoff. The system can be wet or pre-action, single or double interlocked. Heat sensors via a control panel control the automatic valve. During system discharge, when the sensors no longer detect heat, the valve cycles close but will automatically reopen if the sensors' temperature becomes elevated again. There is a minimum discharge timer in the control panel to ensure adequate wetting of the fire with the initial discharge.

The action of the control valve results in a smaller discharge of water into the affected space, with consequent lighter water damage and reduced post-incident cleanup.

11.2.2.6 Water Mist

These systems require addition of a high-pressure pump to the sprinkler system and installation of special application nozzles. Water, under pressures of 175 to 500 psi (12.1 to 34.5 bar), is forced through the specialty nozzles to form extremely small droplets, which remain suspended in the air, effectively performing the identical function of larger droplet sprinklers—absorbing the heat of a fire, thereby depriving it of one of the basic requirements for propagation.

These systems offer the advantage of the commonly available suppression medium while avoiding the hazards to delicate equipment associated with water discharge from standard sprinklers.

11.2.2.7 Foam

Foam and foam-water sprinkler systems are specialized cases of wet sprinkler systems usually reserved for occupancies with high-hazard contents. These systems function by injecting or inducing a concentrated expansion agent into the water flow, resulting in an increase in the discharge's volume of between 20% and 1000%, depending on the particular agent employed. The resultant aggregate of air-filled bubbles flows freely over a burning liquid surface and forms a tough, air-excluding, blanket that seals volatile combustible vapors from access to air. It resists disruption from wind and draft or heat and flame attack and is capable of resealing in case of mechanical rupture. Fire-fighting foams retain these properties for relatively long periods of time. Foams also are defined by expansion and subdivided into three ranges by NFPA 72:

- Low-expansion foam—expansion up to 20
- Medium-expansion foam—expansion from 20 to 200
- High-expansion foam—expansion from 200 to approximately 1000

The following four types of foam systems are permitted:

1. **Fixed System**: an installation in which foam is piped from a central foam station, discharging through fixed delivery outlets to the hazard.
2. **Mobile System**: a type of foam-producing unit that is mounted on wheels and that is self-propelled or towed by a vehicle and can be connected to a water supply or can utilize a premixed foam solution.
3. **Semi-Fixed System**: a system in which the hazard is equipped with fixed discharge outlets connected to piping that terminates at a safe distance.
4. **Portable System**: foam-producing equipment that is transported by hand.

Systems are permitted to be actuated automatically or manually; however, all systems must have provisions for manual actuation.

Foam systems are designed and installed to protect hazards of Class A and Class B fires.

11.2.3 Fire Standpipe Systems

There are three classifications of standpipe systems based on the purpose or intended usage of the system.

1. The Class I standpipe system provides 2 ½ in. hose connections to supply water for use by fire departments and those trained in handling heavy fire streams.
2. The Class II standpipe system provides 1 ½ in. hose stations to supply water for use primarily by the building occupants or by the fire department during initial response.
3. The Class III standpipe system provides 1 ½ in. hose stations to supply water for use by building occupants and 2 ½ in. hose connections to supply a larger volume of water for use by fire departments and those trained in handling heavy fire streams.

11.3 FIRE BARRIER (FIRESTOP) APPLICATION

11.3.1 General

Firestops serve to prevent the propagation of fire and smoke through the openings made to permit mechanical and electrical systems, such as pipe, duct, conduit, and cable tray, pass from one side of a rated partition or floor to the opposite side of the same rated partition or floor.

11.3.2 Firestop System Test Ratings

Firestop systems are tested and rated according to ASTM E814 (UL 1479) to measure and document effectiveness.

1. **F rating:** Represents a minimum amount of time that an installation has been tested to prevent the migration of fire through a particular rated system.
2. **T rating:** Is a measure of the time it takes for any thermocouple on the unexposed side of a rated wall or floor assembly to reach a temperature of 325°F above the temperature of the thermocouple prior to the test.

11.3.3 Firestop Materials

1. **Passive Materials:** Materials that do not react with heat. Passive materials such as sealants, mortars, and foams are considered to be heat sinking or insulating materials and are generally thicker and have limitations on size of the opening and system penetrating the rated partition or floor.
2. **Intumescent Materials:** Materials that expand in volume when exposed to heat or flames exceeding a specified temperature. Intumescent materials can compensate for irregularly sized penetration openings.

11.3.4 Penetration Types and Firestopping Applications

All firestopping system applications are based on penetration type, material, size, and physical characteristics of partition or floor assemblies.

1. Piping generally under 4 in. (102 mm) diameter made of a noncombustible material, such as steel, can use a sealant type of firestopping. Combustible piping, such as plastic pipes, requires intumescent stopping materials as well as smoke seals.
2. Firestopping for duct penetrations without fire dampers depends on the material and shape of the duct. Typical duct firestopping systems include noncombustible flanges to support the wall surface of the duct and the use of intumescent sealant.
3. Cable tray firestopping systems use a combination of intumescent sealants to be injected into the bundle of cable with the use of intumescent putty or pillows between the cable tray and penetration opening.

11.4   MECHANICAL VENTILATION SYSTEMS

11.4.1 Smoke Control Purge Systems

11.4.1.1 Purpose

- Smoke control systems are intended to control and reduce the migration of smoke from the fire/smoke area relative to other areas within the facility and discharge to the exterior.
- A smoke control system
  - enables fire fighters to attack fire quickly,
    - maintains acceptable room conditions for quick and safe egress of occupants during evacuation,
    - reduces smoke damage to equipment and building.
- Consideration should be given to coordination or interface with other life/ property safety systems to complement rather then counteract each system.

11.4.1.2 Ventilation Systems

A ventilation system may consist of an exhaust system and makeup air system. These systems are required to induce a pressure difference between the fire area and adjacent areas to purge smoke. The fire area is typically required to be at a negative pressure relative to adjacent areas. Communicate directly with the Authority Having Jurisdiction to determine smoke purge system requirements in that jurisdiction

Ventilation systems can be dedicated or nondedicated systems.

- Dedicated systems are systems specifically designed with the intent of having a smoke purge system be available 24/7. Scheduled testing should be considered.
- Nondedicated systems utilize and share components with the base building HVAC systems serving the area.

For the protection of electronic equipment, consideration should be given to ensure makeup air is tempered prior to introduction to the fire area. This makeup air can be introduced from adjacent areas or from dedicated air systems serving the fire area.

11.4.1.3 Purge System Controls

The Authority Having Jurisdiction may require a UL-listed annunciator smoke control panel with positive feedback from the base building control system indicating status of purge system operation.

11.4.2 Fire Suppression Purge Systems

11.4.2.1 Purpose

Purge systems are intended to purge chemical clean agent from a room after the required clean agent soak time has expired.

Purge systems

• prevent migration of chemical clean agent to other adjacent rooms and
• minimize clean agent exposure to personnel reentering a room after a clean agent discharge.

11.4.2.2 Interface with Building Ventilation Systems

A ventilation system may consist of an exhaust system and makeup air system. These systems are required to induce a pressure difference between the clean agent area and adjacent areas to purge the chemical. The chemical area must typically be at a negative pressure relative to adjacent areas.

Ventilation systems can be dedicated or nondedicated systems.

• Dedicated systems are systems specifically designed for the purpose of the chemical clean agent purge and must be available 24/7. Scheduled testing should be considered.
• Nondedicated systems utilize and share components with the base building HVAC systems serving the area.

The ventilation rate should be determined in conjunction with the clean agent selected. Refer to the appropriate NFPA section.

11.4.2.3 Interfaces with Fire Suppression Systems

The Authority Having Jurisdiction may require a UL-listed annunciator clean agent purge control panel interfaced with the clean agent fire suppression system, with positive feedback from the base building control system indicating status of purge system operation.

12

Commissioning

12.1   INTRODUCTION

Commissioning of mission critical facilities is an integral part of the process of achieving proper functioning and reliable operation of a facility. Commissioning should commence at project inception, so that owner requirements can be better defined, addressed, and verified throughout the entire design and construction process. Commissioning should include factory acceptance tests, component level tests, system performance tests, and integrated systems tests to verify that the entire infrastructure response to anomalies is in accord with the overall design intent.

The scope for a commissioning project requires increasing involvement toward the end of the project, which unfortunately becomes more difficult as project funding reaches its end. It is not surprising, therefore, that owners often ask the question, "Why should I pay extra to commission a building when my team is already contracted to provide a fully functional facility and a warranty on all systems?" The answer to that question lies in the fact that each building is a unique design, and each design needs to be tested and validated on its own merits. Simply building a facility exactly according to the drawings and specifications does not guarantee that the facility will comply with the owner's requirements.

The commissioning of mission critical facilities encompasses the same philosophy as employed for noncritical facilities (e.g., typical office buildings) but takes it a few extra steps. *ASHRAE Guideline 1-1996, The HVAC Commissioning Process*, defines commissioning as "the process of ensuring that systems are designed, installed, functionally tested, and capable of being operated and maintained to perform in conformity with the design intent" and goes on to state that commissioning "begins with planning and includes design, construction, start-up, acceptance, and training and can be applied throughout the life of the building" (ASHRAE 1996). The Model Commissioning Plan and Guide Specifications published by Portland Energy Conservation, Inc. (PECI), version 2.05 (initially sponsored by the US Department of Energy), defines commissioning as "a systematic process of ensuring that building systems perform interactively according to the design intent and the owner's operational needs" and that this is achieved "beginning in the design phase by documenting the design intent and continuing through construction, acceptance, and the warranty period with actual verification of performance, operation and maintenance (O&M) documentation verification and the training of operating personnel" (PECI 1998)

Though typically associated with new construction projects, commissioning should also be performed on existing facilities following expansions, renovations, or maintenance activities. Owners should consider incorporating aspects of commissioning into their normal operations and maintenance programs as a form of continuous commissioning (or "recommissioning") to ensure that the installed systems and facility operations function and perform to expectations for reliability and availability. Often, when a building's systems drift from their designed operation through lack of maintenance or equipment failure, a program of "retro-commissioning" should be implemented to return the existing systems to proper and efficient operation.

Further information on the commissioning process can be obtained from the *2003 ASHRAE Handbook—HVAC Applications*, chapter 42, "New Building Commissioning" (ASHRAE, 2003d), *ASHRAE Guideline 1-1996, The HVAC Commissioning Process* (ASHRAE 1996), and *ASHRAE Guideline 0-2005, The Commissioning Process* (ASHRAE 2005j).

12.2   PRELIMINARY DOCUMENTATION

For commissioning to be effective it is necessary to define and communicate the facility's intent and performance requirements to the project team. The Owner's Program document, Basis-of-Design document, and the project Commissioning Plan are the best means to accomplish this.

Owner's Program: The Owner's Program document captures the facility's intent (mission) and performance requirements. *ASHRAE Guideline 1-1996* defines the Owner's Program as "the document that outlines the owner's overall vision for the facility and expectations on how it will be used and operated." This document is often prepared by the owner, though frequently it is prepared with the assistance of a program manager or outside consultant to help organize the new facility's program needs, spatial requirements, logistical requirements, etc.

Basis-of-Design: The Basis-of-Design document captures the relevant physical aspects of the facility to achieve the performance requirements in support of the mission (as stated in the Owner's Program document). This document is usually prepared by the architects and engineering consultants hired by the owner and contains a narrative or simplified graphic description of the systems to be designed. This document should be updated through the course of the project, since the means to accomplish the design intent may change based on cost or logistical constraints that could not be identified at the initial phases. As this document is updated to reflect changes implemented in the design of the facility, the resulting changes, especially when they constitute a change in scope, should be checked against the Owner's Program document to ensure that the design intent is still met.

Commissioning Plan: The Commissioning Plan defines the verification and testing process to ensure that the project delivers what is expected, including training, documentation, and project close-out. This Plan is usually prepared by the commissioning agent (CA) who, ideally, should be hired directly by the owner. Without a CA on a project, the Owner's Program and Basis-of-Design documents would probably not be written. Therefore, the CA not only can direct the process of the creation of these documents but can also assist with their creation thereby making certain that each contains information that is transferable to each subsequent step, i.e. first the design process, then the construction, then the testing of the facility and all its systems. In turn, the Commissioning Plan provides the means to verify and test that the entire process and the testing of the installed systems are consistent with the first step of this process, and that is the Owner's Program document.

12.3   COMMISSIONING LEVELS

Commissioning spans the spectrum from the testing of individual components prior to leaving their place of manufacture to simulating catastrophic events upon entire facilities to ensure a myriad of integrated systems perform such that expected responses result in a predicted outcome. A very important aspect of formal commissioning is in compiling, organizing, and recording critical component, equipment, system, and facility information and data in centralized locations to be maintained for the life of the facility. System Manuals that compile information regarding system performance ratings (pressures, flow rates, operating speeds, etc.), sequences of operations for normal, standby, emergency, or other defined modes of operation, maintenance requirements and procedures (spare part lists, maintenance frequencies, critical spares, etc.), and even installation data (vendor contact info, warranty info, etc.) help ensure that operational considerations are not lost during the construction phase. Development of these manuals should begin during the design phase and should be maintained for the life of the facility. New software systems, called building information management systems (BIMS), are being developed specifically for capturing all relevant details of a building or facility and can cross-reference CAD drawings, soft copy documents, locations, spare parts lists, vendors, operating and maintenance procedures, etc., so that these can be used to maximize facility maintenance efforts.

Commissioning activities have been characterized into five broad categories, or levels. Level 1 through Level 3 commissioning is to a large extent focused on the component, assembly, and equipment aspect and ensuring they are procured, received, and installed in accordance with the design documents. Level 4 commissioning is commonly referred to as "site acceptance testing," and Level 5 commissioning is called "integrated systems testing." These levels are summarized as follows:

Level 1: Level 1 commissioning refers to the testing of products prior to leaving their place of manufacture and are sometimes called "factory acceptance tests." The scope and methodology of the proposed tests should ensure they encompass the maximum assurance possible relative to the intended use when installed. This can detect latent bearing defects or minor misalignment conditions that can then be easily resolved prior to shipping. Level 1 commissioning is a good opportunity for the project team to learn about the specified equipment. As good as product cutsheets and catalogs can be, actually seeing, listening, and observing the equipment under operating conditions can provide insight not otherwise obtained. Questions regarding design, operation, maintenance, product support, and customer support can be addressed at the source.

Level 2: Level 2 commissioning refers to field component verification. Products are inspected and verified upon receipt to be as specified and without damage when delivered to the point of use. For critical, expensive, or long-lead-time items, a thorough and comprehensive verification should be considered. Adequate and appropriate on-site transportation and storage should be in place to ensure the product is secured and protected until ready for installation.

Level 3: Level 3 commissioning refers to field inspections and certifications that components are assembled and properly integrated into systems as required by plans and specifications and may be referred to as "system construction verification." These formal progress inspections should be coordinated and documented by the construction manager, led by the architectural and engineering firm(s), and require participation by the owner, contractors, and equipment suppliers. This phase can also include test-fits, mockups, and other work layouts. The operations and maintenance (O&M) staff should be on site at the facility and involved. This allows the O&M staff to become familiar with layouts and configurations, to provide input on maintenance access, stocking, and inventory control of spares, to review installation and O&M manuals, etc., and to question and learn from the design team, construction and installing contractors, and the commissioning agent on how the facility is expected to operate.

Level 4: Level 4 commissioning is commonly called "site acceptance testing" and refers to demonstrating that the related components, equipment, and ancillaries that make up a defined system operate and function to rated, specified, and/or advertised performance criteria. Level 4 commissioning requires that all affected parties understand and agree on how these assembled and installed components are to function and perform as a system. A well thought out commissioning plan during the programming and design phase helps ensure that the design intent and basis-of-design specifications result in contract documents with clear delineation of roles and responsibilities

Level 5: Level 5 commissioning is called "integrated systems tests," where redundant and backup components, systems, and groups of interrelated systems are tested for their response to expected and unexpected anomalies. The challenge of Level 5 commissioning is to ensure that all methods of failure are considered in advance and appropriately tested to demonstrate that the response meets the original programming intent and expectations.

The building automation system (BAS) can play a vital role as a commissioning tool, especially during Level 4 and Level 5 tests. Obviously, the BAS system itself must first be subjected to a rigorous commissioning process (to ensure valid and accurate data collection, i.e., point to point verification) prior to use in commissioning other systems. This creates a project "critical-path" challenge in that the BAS system typically lags the other systems' design and installation phases. The critical infrastructure needs to be selected and designed before the BAS design can be completed, and the infrastructure and related equipment must be installed before the BAS installation. Yet, the start-up and commissioning of the BAS system must occur before it can be utilized to support commissioning of the monitored and controlled systems.

12.4 COMMISSIONING MISSION CRITICAL FACILITIES

Mission critical facilities typically include more demanding performance requirements regarding how they are to respond to expected and unexpected anomalies without impacting "critical" operations. Systems usually include redundant components and utility feeds and excess capacity or backup systems or equipment that can be automatically or manually activated during emergency modes to protect the "mission." These redundant or backup components, systems, or groups of inter-related systems are tested during Level 5 integrated systems tests. It is Level 5 commissioning that typically sets mission critical facilities apart from commissioning for typical office buildings.

Before an effective level 5 commissioning plan can be developed, it is fundamental that acceptance criteria be established that are founded in ensuring the facility can perform reliably to protect the mission from expected internal and external anomalies. For level 5 commissioning to be successful, it should begin with the project programming phase where the effort to be expended on quality assurance is weighed against the criticality of the mission, the complexity of the facility, and the resources available. Inevitably, as the project progresses and pressures mount to control costs and improve the schedule, the commitment to commissioning will be tested.

Level 5 commissioning is where the facility is shown to be capable of meeting the design intent and program requirements. Examples of Level 5 commissioning would include loss of normal power tests coupled with UPS and emergency generator operations. Uninterruptible power supply (UPS) systems may be load tested from incoming "utility" power down to the remote power panels (RPPs) including the UPS modules and power distribution units (PDUs). Not only would the system be subjected to full loading via load banks, but the system also would be tested to respond to various failure modes, such as loss of incoming power (battery run for static UPSs), module failures (step load increases for multiple module configurations), and other similar performance tests. The heat rejected by the load banks can provide cooling loads for the associated HVAC and equipment cooling systems. The BAS monitoring, control, and alert systems are verified as well. A good strategy is to overlay as many interrelated systems tests as possible.

12.5 COMMISSIONING COSTS

Level 1 activities typically occur at the manufacturer's expense and, except where witnessing by the owner is required or where testing or documentation of testing is specified beyond the standard manufacturer's quality assurance/quality control (QA/QC) process, the costs are included in the equipment pricing.

Level 2 activities, or "receiving" type inspections, require some additional paperwork to formalize what are typical receiving processes and procedures and carry relatively small additional costs.

Typical costs incurred for Level 3 activities—where construction managers, architects, and/or engineers conduct inspections to ensure means and methods are performed in accordance with design specifications and drawings and with acceptable quality—are also included in construction projects. Formal commissioning plans tend to increase the level of scrutiny, documentation, and accountability of these efforts, and so incremental increases in both time and costs should be expected.

Obviously, Level 4 commissioning requires significantly more planning, more detailed procedures, more time and manpower, and, of course, higher overall costs than traditional start-up and testing activities. The assurance resulting from Level 4 commissioning that critical systems will perform safely and as intended is necessary, and essentially a prerequisite to attempting Level 5 integrated systems testing. As with any worthwhile testing of new systems, failures can occur, resulting in delays and remediation (varying from adjustments, to repairs, to even redesign and modification). The project budget and schedule should include contingencies (time and money) during the Level 4 commissioning to address and resolve discrepancies and unexpected re-work.

For Level 5 commissioning to produce positive results, it first requires a high degree of Level 1 through Level 4 commissioning as a foundation. Just as it is better to identify faulty components prior to shipping, to identify damaged deliveries prior to installation, and to identify installation errors prior to system start-up, it is better to identify system-level issues prior to attempting integrated systems testing. Also, as the costs of commissioning efforts tend to increase (especially from the owner's perspective) as the "level" increases, Level 5 commissioning can be quite expensive in both time and money.

12.6 SUMMARY

Most facilities undergo some degree of commissioning as part of the owner's acceptance process. Mission critical facilities require more thorough and comprehensive testing to ensure continuous operations. MCF commissioning requires demonstrating that redundant, back-up, and interrelated systems automatically recognize and respond to expected and unexpected anomalies.

Costs of formal commissioning can be significant. They will increase as a percentage of the overall project budget as the criticality and complexity of the site infrastructure increase. This is especially true of the Leve 4 and Level 5 commissioning activities.

The higher the owner's expectation that the facility perform reliably to support a critical mission, the more effort and resources should be dedicated to a thorough and comprehensive commissioning program. The more sophisticated and complex the facility and associated infrastructure, the more complex and demanding the commissioning program becomes. As with any effective quality assurance program, commissioning should ultimately pay far more dividends than the initial investment.

Table 12.1 Categories of Formal Commissioning Activities

Level	Name	Description
1	Factory acceptance tests	Product testing and verification to ensure compliance with manufacturer's advertised specifications, ratings, and characteristics. These can be augmented to include any owner-defined functional, performance, or aesthetic requirements and can include component certifications or documentation. Sometimes referred to as "factory witness tests" when the tests must be performed in the presence of an owner's representative.
2	Field component verification	Inspection, verification, or tests performed on the products upon delivery to the site to ensure the products delivered match those purchased and tested during the factory acceptance tests and have not been damaged or altered during shipment.
3	System construction verification	Field inspections and certifications that components are assembled into systems as required by plans and specifications. Includes verifying compliance with specified means and methods, accessibility, maintainability, and manufacturer's installation requirements and directives.
4	Site acceptance testing	Demonstration that related components, equipment, and ancillaries of a defined system operate and function to acceptance criteria. This should include normal, maintenance, and emergency modes of operation, verifying settings, safeties, and capacities, and performance of associated monitoring and control functions.
5	Integrated systems testing	The functional performance testing of interrelated components and systems to respond as intended to expected and unexpected anomalies.

13

Availability and Redundancy

It is extremely important to understand the concept of availability when considering HVAC systems for datacom facilities. Mission critical datacom facilities, as their name implies, are required to run 24 hours a day, 7 days a week, year-round, and any disruption to that operation typically results in a loss of service/revenue for the end user. This may violate the service level agreement (SLA) between the facility operator and the end user.

The high heat density of the equipment combined with its thermal sensitivity is a volatile combination, and any loss or disruption to cooling or humidity control, even for a very short period or time, can lead to equipment damage and/or loss of data. New IT hardware provides the end user with the ability to monitor internal temperatures, and they may become aware of a cooling problem before the facility operator. Even at moderate heat densities (1.5 kW per rack or 50 W per ft^2), the resulting temperature gradient (measured as an average over the first 20 minutes of a complete cooling outage) is on the order of 2.5°F per minute (Telcordia 2001). This gradient exceeds all known electronic equipment warranty specifications.

13.1 AVAILABILITY DEFINITIONS

Availability is a percentage value representing the degree to which a system or component is operational and accessible when required for use (IEEE 1990). Availability typically accounts for component and system maintenance (Beaty 2004a). Values of 99.999% ("five nines") and higher are commonly referenced in the electrical design of datacom facilities but are difficult to attain. Availability of 100% can never be guaranteed. For individual components, the availability is often determined through field data. Failure prediction of components should be utilized, and maintenance should be performed before predicted failures can occur. For assemblies and systems, availability is often the result of a mathematical evaluation based on the availability of individual components and any redundancy or diversity that may be employed. Availability is composed of two variables, mean time between failure (MTBF) and mean time to repair (MTTR). MTBF is a basic measure of a system's reliability but means little without providing a definition of failure. Typically, it means the loss of critical processing equipment. Mean time to repair (MTTR) is the expected time to recover a system from a failure and is equally important because the time to recover could be much greater than the time for service personnel to respond. Together, these two factors attempt to quantify the expected availability of a critical system or, in other words, its expected uptime.

The formula below illustrates how both MTBF and MTTR impact the overall availability of a system. As the MTBF goes up, availability goes up. As the MTTR goes up, availability goes down.

$$\text{Availability} = \frac{MTBF}{(MTBF + MTTR)}$$

Fault tree analysis can help detail the path of events, both normal and fault related, that lead down to the component-level fault or undesired event that is being investigated (top-to-bottom approach). Reliability is calculated by converting a completed fault tree into an equivalent set of equations. This is done using the algebra of events, also referred to as Boolean algebra.

FMEA (failure mode and effects analysis) is a process used for analyzing the failure modes of a system. This information is then used to determine the impact each failure would have on the system, thereby leading to an improved system design. The analysis can go a step further by assigning a severity level to each of the failure modes in which case it would be called a FMECA (failure mode, effects and criticality analysis). FMEA uses a bottom-to-top approach. For instance, the analysis starts with the individual components and works its way up to the entire system. Apart from being used as a design tool, it can be used to calculate the reliability of the overall system.

In these types of analyses, however, probability data needed for the calculations can be difficult to obtain for various pieces of equipment, which is why availability calculations for HVAC systems are seldom done. Published data on components and systems are not readily available, and defining a cooling failure is difficult. For instance, when IT equipment completely loses power, it turns off. This is clearly a failure. But when cooling fails, the IT equipment can remain operational for as long as the inlet temperature and humidity remain within allowable limits. This may or may not be defined as a failure.

Cooling is an area where further research is needed to allow for the calculation of system availability as a function of component availability and level of redundancy. However, overall data center reliability cannot be calculated from a mechanical system point of view alone. A holistic approach is required in which the probabilities of N number of modes of failure (mechanical, electrical, plumbing, structural, human element, etc.) are calculated as though each mode of failure is in series with any other mode of failure. If the uptime of a mechanical system were to be calculated to be 99.99% (which is difficult to achieve), then it could never be said that the anticipated uptime for the overall facility would also be 99.99%. This approach doesn't account for the fact that the other systems have a finite probability that is in series with the mechanical systems' probability.

Until reliability data on cooling equipment become available, the operator should focus on known best practices such as good monitoring and system design, operation and maintenance (see section 13.5, "Practical Examples").

13.2 REDUNDANCY

System availability may be so vital that the potential cost of system failure will justify redundant systems, capacity, and/or components, as well as increased diversity.

The most common method used to attain greater system availability is to add redundant parallel components to avoid having a single component failure trigger a system-wide failure. When dealing with redundancy in HVAC systems the terms $N+1$, $N+2$, and $2N$ are commonly used to indicate how many additional components are to be provided. N represents the number of pieces of equipment needed to satisfy the normal load. Redundant equipment is necessary to compensate for failed equipment and provide an opportunity for maintenance while the remaining online capacity supports the normal load.

In the case of datacom facilities utilizing CRAC units, if $N+1$ redundancy is required, a determination would first be made as to how many units are required to satisfy the normal (N) cooling load. One additional unit would then be provided to achieve $N+1$ redundancy.

As the requirements for the degree of availability increase, so too should the level of redundancy of the equipment. Data correlating the degrees of availability and redundancy are not available, but in general, a Class 3 or Class 4 facility would not have any cooling redundancy (N), a Class 2 facility would have $N+1$ cooling redundancy, and a Class 1 facility would have at least $N+2$ cooling redundancy. These levels of redundancy are rules of thumb, and actual designed redundancy is usually selected based on the anecdotal evidence and experience of the users, IT managers, facilities staff, and engineers.

The heat density and resultant rate of temperature rise in the event of a loss of cooling should also be a consideration when determining the degree of redundancy required. If heat density is so low that a loss of a cooling unit in an N configuration only results in a small temperature rise in any area of the space, this may be acceptable. However, in cases of high heat density there may be cases where a loss of cooling can result in a very high rate of change of temperature in a certain area. Even if the resultant temperature is still within allowable limits, the allowable rate of change of temperature may be exceeded. This can be avoided by ensuring that the loss of any cooling unit does not result in an unallowable rate of change of temperature. This may have more of an effect on redundancy than keeping the absolute temperature within allowable limits.

While in theory redundancy can be achieved with N+1 (or more air-handling or CRAC units), the dynamics of underfloor and overhead flow are such that the loss of a specific unit can be critical for a specific area. Redundancy should be confirmed during the commissioning phase of the project. CFD analysis may also be performed to determine the impact of losing specific units in critical use areas. For large spaces, consider using N+1 for every X number of units so as to provide one redundant unit for every set of X units required. Each set of units controls an individual zone of the data center.

Care should be taken to exercise redundant equipment frequently to prevent conditions that enhance the growth of mold and mildew in filters, insulated unit enclosures, and outside air pathways where spores and food sources for microbial growth may accumulate. Another approach is to keep redundant equipment operational at all times but use variable-frequency drives (VFDs) to control fan speed. In this manner, the fans operate at a speed to match loads. If a fan fails, the other fans ramp up to maintain the required airflows. No schedule is required for exercising equipment since all equipment is operational (unless loads are so low that it is not practical to operate all equipment). Care should be taken to ensure that redundancy truly exists at minimum airflow conditions (possibly using CFD or actual test methods) and that sensible heat ratio doesn't decrease to the point that a large amount of dehumidification (and subsequent need to rehumidify) is occurring.

Exercising the liquid side of the CRAC units is also important. Chilled water or water/glycol cooled DX units should have their control valves cycled open periodically to allow flow and prevent sludge buildup and corrosion inside the piping.

13.3 DIVERSITY

Systems that employ an alternate path for distribution are said to have diversity. One company has developed a tiered classification system to rank the level of diversity and redundancy in a data center design (Turner 2003). A Tier I facility would have only one power distribution path with no redundancy, Tier II also has only one distribution path but there is N+1 redundancy in that path, Tier III has two power distribution paths with one active and one passive, and Tier IV would have two completely independent active power distribution paths sharing the critical load equally. The calculated availability for each of these tiers ranges from 99.671% for Tier I to 99.995% for Tier IV. Even with a Tier IV design, it isn't possible to reach the goal of "five nines" or 99.999% availability, due to human involvement. The calculation for Tier IV assumes one site outage, such as a fire alarm or emergency power off (EPO) event, every five years.

With dual feeds, it is often possible to perform planned information technology equipment (ITE) air-moving device infrastructure activity without shutting down critical loads, a concept called "concurrently maintainable." Criteria have been developed for certification of "fault tolerant" equipment that can be fed by dual power sources (Brill 2002).

13.4 HUMAN ERROR AND AVAILABILITY

System simplicity and ease of operation should be a constant consideration, as a substantial percentage of reported data center failures have been related to human error. The most robust data center design can be compromised by human error. Regardless of the reason for system failures, the data center availability is affected. Causes for human error can include poor documentation, lack of training, lack of understanding, or even fatigue during long periods of after-hours maintenance. Human error can be minimized by designing equipment and systems to be fail-safe by ensuring that operator actions are deliberate and by limiting access to systems to trained personnel only. Training should start during the commissioning phase and should continue throughout the life of the facility.

Well established and documented procedures can also help prevent human error. Examples of these include:

*   Tag-in/tag-out procedures to reduce the chances of opening or closing valves or switches that should not be exercised under certain circumstances
*   Scripting procedures, or critical environment work authorizations (CEWA), for all work in critical environments
*   Requirement for two signatures of building engineers or facility managers for any change of state, such as opening or closing valves, turning equipment on or off, etc.

These measures don't eliminate the possibility of human error, but they do address most of the failures caused by thoughtless or careless actions.

Sabotage and terrorism are not human errors per se, but they are events that can occur and should be protected against. Facilities should have security policies that limit personnel having access to the facility. Outdoor equipment such as condensers and cooling towers should also be isolated to limit access to only those authorized to maintain and operate them.

13.5 PRACTICAL EXAMPLES

Practical applications to increase HVAC system availability for datacom facility design may include any of the items listed below. The following are just examples.

*   Backup utilities: power generation, second electric service, water supply, fuel supply, etc. Emergency power supplies will probably need to feed some aspects of HVAC systems as well as datacom equipment to allow for continuous equipment operation within allowable environmental conditions
*   Backup air-moving equipment: air handlers, fans, computer room units, etc.
*   Backup and/or cross-connected cooling equipment: chillers, pumps, cooling towers, dry coolers, cooling coils, makeup water supply, etc.
*   Diverse piping systems, chilled water, condenser water, etc.

- Full or partial backup of air-moving and/or cooling equipment on emergency power
- Backup thermal storage: chilled water, ice, makeup water, etc.
- Alternate power sources for A/C equipment
- Utilize IT equipment with dual power supplies so that two power sources can be connected and there is no interruption in power if one of the sources fails.
- Monitoring of temperatures for early warning of component failures
- Maintain spare parts inventory on site
- Provide temporary cooling equipment for fast deployment
- Document emergency response plans
- Use leak detection systems with alarms monitored remotely
- Maintain documentation with the locations of all isolation valves.
- Keep systems, especially controls and automation, as simple as possible. The more complex the systems are, the greater the chances of failure and the longer the time to recover.

14

Energy Efficiency

14.1 INTRODUCTION

Energy is an important metric because energy usage in telecommunications and data centers is a significant portion of facility operating costs. Energy efficiency considerations covered in this chapter fall into four categories: environmental criteria, generation, distribution, and other measures. Subcategories of "generation" include chilled-water plants; CRAC units; fans, pumps, and variable-speed drives; humidity control; water-side economizers; air-side economizers; outdoor air ventilation; and part-load operation. Subcategories of "distribution" include in-room airflow distribution, CRAC units—distribution, and part-load operation—distribution. Subcategories of "other measures" include datacom equipment energy usage, UPS energy efficiency, emerging technologies, controls and energy management, and system energy simulation.

ASHRAE's Standard 90.1 (ASHRAE 2004i) provides minimum requirements for the energy efficiency of almost all nonresidential facilities, including data centers. This includes efficiency standards for the building envelope, HVAC systems, service water heating, and lighting. Much of the energy usage in a data center, however, is consumed directly by the datacom equipment in the space. The space environmental conditions, the design and configuration of the cooling system, and the control protocol used to cool this equipment can result in dramatic differences in energy consumption, even if the listed efficiency of the HVAC equipment is identical from one case to another. As such, an extended discussion of energy efficiency, specific to data centers, is warranted.

Case studies of energy consumption in datacom facilities have been inventoried and are available for public review (LBNL 2003). A summary of existing research regarding energy efficiency in datacom facilities and a roadmap for further research in this area have also been published (Tschudi 2003). Areas covered include monitoring and control, electrical systems, and HVAC systems, including free cooling, and use of variable-capacity compressors in CRAC units.

14.2   ENVIRONMENTAL CRITERIA

Chapter 2 of ASHRAE's *Thermal Guidelines for Data Processing Environments* (ASHRAE 2004h) recommends that the temperature in a data center be kept between 68°F (20°C) and 77°F (25°C) and that the relative humidity be kept between 40% RH and 55% RH. For the telecommunications industry, Telcordia GR-3028 (Telcordia 2001) recommends as an appropriate (based on economic considerations) facility operating temperature 65°F-80°F (18°C-27°C) and maximum relative humidity of 55%.

The "traditional" temperature/humidity tolerance of data centers has been ±2°F (1.1°C) dry bulb and ±5% relative humidity. This range, however, is much more stringent than the operating requirements for most datacom equipment.

Relaxation of stringent environmental conditions, and adoption of a broader environmental range, such as that found in *Thermal Guidelines* (ASHRAE 2004h), provides for substantial energy savings due to the following:

- **Thermodynamic efficiency of vapor compression cycles can be increased:** Raising the space temperature allows the vapor compression cycle to run with a smaller temperature differential. This increases the thermodynamic efficiency of the cycle. With chilled-water plants, the rule-of-thumb increase in efficiency is 1%-3% for every 1°F (0.6°C) rise in evaporator temperature. Chiller part-load efficiencies in the range of 0.20 kW/ton are possible with 60°F (16°C) chilled water and concurrent low condenser water temperature. In many climates, it may be possible to produce 60°F (16°C) water through evaporative cooling without the use of chillers for many hours of the year.

- **Humidification load is decreased:** The humidification load is decreased both by the decrease in the minimum relative humidity level (from 45% to 40% RH) and also by the decrease in the lower limit for temperature. For example, the design humidification load for a 68°F (20°C)/40% RH condition (40.7 grains per pound of outdoor air) is only about 70% of the load for the condition of 72°F (22°C)/50% (58.5 grains per pound). Actual annual humidification energy savings will be even greater since the baseline (outdoor) humidity is not zero and varies over the course of the humidification season. A dew-point bin data analysis would be needed for the locality in question to determine actual savings.

- **Dehumidification load is decreased:** Often, dehumidification in telecommunications and data center environments occurs through use of the cooling coil in CRAC units. Typically the cooling coil temperature is dropped if dehumidification is required because this increases the amount of condensation on the coil and decreases space absolute humidity. Since the cooler coil can result in overcooling of the space, the colder discharge air is often reheated in constant-volume systems, resulting in high energy use through simultaneous heating and cooling. Increasing the maximum relative humidity level will reduce the number of hours that the cooling coil is operating in the dehumidification mode and, thus, the need for simultaneous heating and cooling.

• Some European telecommunications firms have been able to eliminate refrigerant-based cooling systems either most of the time or entirely by (aggressively) allowing the space temperature and humidity to vary through the full range of allowable equipment operating environments. These facilities utilize 100% outdoor air (direct free cooling), some or all of the time, in combination with detailed space environmental design using CFD techniques. The environmental system energy usage of these facilities is claimed to be less than 50% of the energy usage of a system utilizing refrigerant-based cooling (Cinato 1998; Kiff 1995).

• For certain equipment facilities, however, a wider temperature range may lead to increased operating costs. Two major costs associated with the operation of telecommunications huts and vaults are those for HVAC energy use and battery replacement. Based on HVAC energy costs and battery costs alone, lowering the maximum operating temperature in huts and vaults is economically advantageous—the decrease in battery costs more than offsets the increase in HVAC energy costs (Herrlin 1998).

14.3 CHILLED-WATER PLANTS

Chilled-water plants typically include the following energy-consuming equipment: chillers, chilled-water pumps, condenser water pumps, and cooling tower fans. In addition, they may include passive devices such as heat exchangers for free cooling. Pipes, valves, and control systems are also part of the system. The intent of this discussion is not to describe chilled-water plants, which are described more fully in chapter 4, "Computer Room Cooling Overview," but rather to indicate the energy efficiency considerations and methodologies that can be used to provide chilled water in an efficient yet reliable manner. The most significant increases in plant efficiency have typically been attributed to raising chilled-water temperatures and to implementing variable-speed control of prime movers such as chiller compressors, fans, and pumps.

14.3.1 Water Chillers

Chillers can be first categorized by type of heat rejection: air or water. If available, water-cooled chillers almost always result in higher efficiency because wet-bulb temperatures are lower than dry-bulb temperatures and the lower heat rejection temperature results in higher thermodynamic efficiency.

The three main types of water-cooled chillers typically found in a central plant are centrifugal, reciprocating, or screw. Ratings can be obtained based on full load, a specific part-load condition, or as an integrated part load value (IPLV) based on ARI 550/590-98 (ARI 1998). Air-cooled chillers are typically reciprocating, scroll, or screw.

Full- and part-load efficiencies can vary greatly from one manufacturer to another and can also vary greatly depending on the exact design conditions, so it always makes sense to obtain project-specific selections from several manufacturers. The following points should be considered.

- There is a wide range of efficiency depending on the type of chiller. Choose a chiller optimized for the project. Consider the most probable part-load operating condition in the selection.
- Look at the effect of chilled water and condenser water temperatures (and temperature differentials) on chiller efficiency.
- Chillers that have variable-frequency drives typically have very good part-load efficiency curves.
- Chillers that allow for variable flow though the evaporator can result in lower pumping and installation costs relative to a primary/secondary chilled-water pumping system.

14.3.2 Chilled-Water Pumps

There are several considerations for chilled-water pump selection.

- The pump selection should be optimized for the operating point. Check several manufacturers and pump models to find the most efficient pump for the application.
- The delta T of the chilled water should be optimized. A greater delta T will result in lower flow and, thus, lower pumping energy consumption but potentially lower chiller efficiency or larger chilled-water coils.
- Premium efficiency motors and, where applicable, variable-speed drives should be specified.

14.3.3 Condenser Water Pumps

There are several considerations for condenser water pump selection.

- The pump selection should be optimized for the operating point.
- The delta T of the condenser water should be optimized. A greater delta T will result in lower pumping costs but potentially lower chiller efficiency.
- Premium efficiency motors and, where applicable, variable-speed drives should be specified.

14.3.4 Cooling Towers

Several strategies can be used to minimize energy consumption in cooling towers. They include the following:

- Tower fan energy consumption can be quite variable for a given cooling load. Check several vendors, and several tower models from each vendor, to optimize tower selection for efficient operation.

- For choice of fan, propeller fans typically have lower unit energy consumption than centrifugal fans.
- Towers designed for a high turndown ratio can allow for condenser water flow better matched to chiller needs, especially in plants with multiple chillers.
- Premium efficiency motors and variable-speed drives should be specified.
- Operating multiple towers through the use of variable-frequency drives may be more efficient than operating a single tower at full fan speed, due to fan cube laws.

14.3.5 Controls

Proper control is an essential part of an efficiently operated chilled-water plant. The following points need to be carefully considered:

- The part-load operating mix of equipment should be optimized for minimal energy consumption. A chiller plant optimization study may be required to determine the best mix of equipment to operate at any given part-load condition.
- Pumping strategies should be optimized for efficient part-load operation
- Chilled water and condenser water temperature reset should be optimized
- Tower fan speed should be optimized for efficient part-load operation
- Precooling and free-cooling setpoints should be optimized

14.3.6 System Simulation and Optimization

Once the full-load and part-load conditions are known during the design stage of a project, a chilled-water plant model should be created with an energy simulation program to simulate facility operation for a full calendar year. This model can be used to optimize parameters such as chilled water supply and return temperatures, condenser water supply, the addition of heat exchangers for precooling or free cooling of chilled water, etc. Due to the wide distribution of wet- and dry-bulb temperatures in the United States (and the world), a design optimized for one climate is rarely the best design for another locale. If the program is sophisticated enough, energy usage can be optimized as a function of outdoor air wet-bulb (or dry-bulb for air-cooled chillers) temperature. ASHRAE provides extensive guidance on optimization in the *2003 ASHRAE Handbook—HVAC Applications*, chapter 41, "Supervisory Control Strategies and Optimization" (ASHRAE 2003c).

14.4 CRAC UNITS: GENERATION

Computer room air-conditioning (CRAC) units are popular for conditioning and control of datacom facilities. Rating of CRAC units, including energy efficiency ratings, is covered by ASHRAE Standard 127 (ASHRAE 2001). Energy-consuming components in CRAC units may include any of the following:

- Compressors
- Fan systems
- Reheat components (can be electric, hot water, hot gas)
- Humidifiers (several types are available)
- Heat rejection devices (usually a dedicated remote condenser, dry cooler, or wet cooler)

The following energy efficiency considerations should be made:

- The thermodynamic efficiency of a central plant (especially a water-cooled plant) is usually much higher than the efficiency of a compressor found in the typical 10-60 ton CRAC unit.
- CRAC unit reheat coils are almost never required in an efficiently designed system.
- If dry coolers or wet coolers are installed, water-side economizer coils can be installed to minimize system energy use in most climates (the fan energy increase must be compared to reduced compressor energy use, which is site specific). The efficiency gains are greatest if the compressors are specified with cylinder unloading when the economizer coil is working at partial load.
- Wet coolers are preferred over dry coolers, as the water spray over the cooler reduces the required fan energy.
- There is significant variation in the power consumption of the different humidification systems. Since data centers typically require cooling year-round, ultrasonic systems will generally be the most energy efficient, as adiabatic cooling of the airstream occurs as part of the humidification process. Humidification systems that may carry over impurities to the supply air should be avoided.

14.5   FANS, PUMPS, AND VARIABLE-SPEED DRIVES

Fans and pumps (for chilled-water systems) are some of the largest users of energy in a data center. One benchmark study that examined several data centers found that air movement costs as a percentage of overall energy costs typically varied between 5% and 12% (LBNL 2005). As such, careful design of fans and pumps in a data center and use of variable-speed drives to allow for energy-efficient part-load operation are particularly important.

14.5.1   Fans

The air horsepower, or the theoretical power required to drive a 100% mechanically efficient fan, is linearly proportional to both the flow rate and the total pressure across the fan.

Methods to minimize the energy consumption of fan systems in data centers include the following:

• Minimizing pressure drop through use of larger ducts, raised-floor or overhead air spaces, coils, and heat exchangers (including cooling towers), though possibly having a higher initial cost, will lower energy operating costs and quickly justify any added expense. By lowering air system resistance, smaller fans and motors can be used, which will provide offsetting capital expense reduction.

• Air leakage is a major source of wasted energy. Raised floors can be leaky and require additional airflow, resulting in higher energy costs. Sealing of openings in the floor, such as cable tray penetrations, can result in lower airflow. Generally, CRAC units should be sized to deliver more air than the amount calculated as flow through floor tiles, and an engineered analysis of leakage rates can provide the necessary cooling airflow yet keep fan energy consumption to a minimum.

• Fan speed should be adjusted during commissioning to match the system requirements. Caution is required on DX units to minimize the chance of freezing the coil.

• Two-speed or variable-speed fans can reduce energy consumption during part-load operation.

• Premium efficiency motors should be specified.

• Fans should be selected for maximum operating efficiency. Fans with low face velocity should be considered if the fan discharge is a poor one to minimize discharge losses.

• Filters should be selected to provide the needed filtration with a minimum pressure drop. Regular maintenance of the filters will help to maintain low pressure drop.

14.5.2 Pumps

The water horsepower, or the theoretical power required to drive a 100% mechanically efficient pump, is also linearly proportional to both the flow rate and the total pressure across the pump.

Methods to minimize the energy consumption of pump systems in data centers include the following:

• Minimizing system pressure drop through use of larger pipes, minimizing run lengths and direction changes, use of long radius bends, and minimizing pressure drop in heat exchangers can improve system efficiency.

• Premium efficiency motors should be specified

• Pumps should be selected for maximum operating efficiency.

• Two-speed or variable-speed pumps can reduce energy consumption during part-load operation. To take advantage of this part-load energy efficiency, two-way chilled-water valves should be specified.

- The overall pumping system should be designed for maximum efficiency. This may include designs that eliminate bypasses, use only primary pumps with VFDs, etc.

14.5.3 Variable-Speed Drives

A review of fan laws (ASHRAE 2004c) and pump laws (ASHRAE 2004g) shows that the power input to both fans and pumps is proportional to the cube of the speed of these devices. As such, a fan or pump operating at 50% of its normal speed requires only 12.5% of the theoretical power of the same device operating at 100% speed. The energy-saving potential of variable-speed drives thus becomes quite apparent when a device can operate at part load.

14.6 HUMIDITY CONTROL

A significant percentage of the energy bill of a data center can be spent on humidification and dehumidification.

The main opportunity for energy reduction from humidification is a reduction in the required setpoint. This has already been discussed in section 14.2.

Another opportunity for cost reduction is to compare the fuel cost for different steam systems: steam generated from a gas-based steam boiler will generally cost less per pound than steam from an electric boiler or other electric source. However, humidification systems that may carry over impurities to the supply air must be avoided.

It is important to keep in mind that telecommunications and data centers typically do not have an internal source for humidity. Outdoor air, either forced or infiltration, is the cause of changes in the absolute humidity in the space. Reductions in infiltration and/or the rate of ventilation, therefore, directly affect the amount of humidification required in a space. It has been reported that a data center with tight construction can maintain humidity levels for several days if the outdoor air is concurrently shut off (Conner 1988).

Datacom systems contain components that are sensitive to electrostatic discharge (ESD). Associated failures are more likely to occur at low relative humidity. Some central offices, especially those in regions with dry climates and/or cold winters, may be humidified. A major reason for humidification is to reduce the costs associated with failures caused by ESD.

ESD failures are costly, but humidification is not necessarily a cost-effective solution. Telcordia research indicates that steam humidification to a 30% setpoint results in increased net costs in all US climates. At a 15% setpoint, humidification may be marginally cost-effective in cold climates, providing that humidification equipment is already installed and maintenance costs are low. Other approaches can better be used to reduce ESD failures, notably grounding of personnel (Herrlin 1996). Generally accepted telecom practice is not to actively humidify the central office.

14.6.1 Dehumidification

Dehumidification is most typically accomplished by use of cooling coils, which condense excess moisture out of the air by operating below the dew point of the air passing through the coil. The cooling coil thus typically performs the dual function of cooling and dehumidifying. One problem with this approach is that the optimal temperature for cooling may not be the required temperature for dehumidification. If dehumidification requires a lower temperature, the air is subcooled and typically reheated, wasting energy. Dehumidification systems should be designed to avoid the need to reheat under low-load conditions.

Several approaches can be taken to help resolve the energy wasted with simultaneous (or sequential) heating and cooling. A variable air volume (VAV) approach is one method, if the cooling equipment and the overall system can adopt this approach without a deleterious effect on the operation of the overall system. By reducing the volume of air through the coil, an airflow level can be reached where the amount of sensible and latent cooling is satisfied with the same airflow and coil temperature. The need to reheat the air to avoid overcooling is thereby eliminated. Another approach is to use a split-coil design, whereby a call for dehumidification results in a solenoid valve closing refrigerant to one-third of the coil with the other two-thirds of the coil operating at a lower surface temperature. This provides for a lower sensible heat ratio, thus allowing for increased dehumidification without overcooling the space or requiring reheat.

An alternative method is to perform all dehumidification in a makeup air or independent recirculation system for the space. As long as space pressurization eliminates infiltration, the makeup air system can dehumidify. Since telecommunications and data centers typically do not have an internal source for humidity, the absolute humidity of the makeup air system, often referred to as dew-point control, can be maintained in the space (Conner 1988).

Yet another method of dehumidification is the use of desiccant or other technologies for the removal of excess moisture. Providing an independent system for dehumidification frees up the cooling coil to perform its primary function (cooling) and again eliminates the need for simultaneous heating and cooling. Various configurations of desiccant wheels, in conjunction with enthalpy wheels, sensible wheels, and bypass, are covered in Wong et al. (2002). A metric called the SEVLI, or Source Energy Ventilation Load Index, is used to compare the source energy of various configurations. Results for Atlanta showed that the SEVLI for an enthalpy wheel assisted vapor compression system was 2.3 times the SEVLI for an enthalpy-wheel assisted desiccant system.

14.7 WATER-SIDE ECONOMIZERS

Water-side economizers use cool outdoor dry- or wet-bulb conditions to generate condenser water that can partially or fully meet the facility's cooling requirements. There are two basic types of water-side economizers: direct and indirect free cooling. In a direct system, the condenser water is circulated directly through the chilled-water circuit. In an indirect system, a heat exchanger is added to separate the condenser-water and chilled-water loops. For comparison, Figure 14.1 shows a schematic of a direct water-side economizer and Figure 14.2 shows a schematic of an indirect water-side ecomonizer.

Water-cooled chilled-water plants incorporating water-side economizers often use the indirect approach. This approach allows the chilled-water plant cooling towers to generate cold condenser water whenever ambient wet-bulb temperatures permit. This cold condenser water is then passed through a heat exchanger where it is used to absorb the heat from the chilled-water loop. When the condenser water is cold enough that it can fully meet the cooling load, the water chillers can be shut off. In order to fully meet data center cooling loads, outdoor wet bulbs generally have to be 7°F-10°F (4°C-6°C) less than the design chilled-water temperature, depending on the approach temperature of the tower and the design temperature rise across the heat exchanger.

Water-side economizers used in conjunction with central chilled-water plants can be arranged either in series or parallel. When arranged in parallel, the chillers are shut off and the economizers' heat exchanger is enabled when the outdoor wet-bulb temperatures are low enough to allow full cooling through the heat exchanger. When arranged in series, condenser water is routed through the heat exchanger whenever the ambient wet-bulb temperature is low enough to allow a portion of the cooling load to be met by the heat exchanger. In this mode, condenser water flows through both the heat exchanger and chiller in series, resulting in significantly more "free cooling" hours, with the only additional energy expense being the energy required to pump water through both the heat exchanger and the chiller. Once the wet-bulb conditions permit full cooling by the heat exchanger, flow can bypass the chiller evaporator, reducing pumping head and increasing energy efficiency. Water-side economizers, when used in conjunction with water-cooled chilled-water plants, require heat exchangers, larger cooling towers, and possibly additional pumps (depending upon the piping arrangement). Additionally, the economizers require motorized control valves to divert the direction of the water flow to the heat exchanger as required. These changes of valve position, if programmed to perform automatically, are likely to occur often in a moderate climate, especially when the heat exchanger is piped in the series arrangement. Frequent changes of state may need to be monitored to ensure reliable transition from compressor cooling to free cooling.

Direct water-side economizer operation can take a number of forms. One of the most common in the data center environment is the "dry cooler" used in conjunction with a water-cooled air conditioner. This direct system can use a fan-powered air-to-liquid heat exchanger (dry cooler) to cool the condenser water using outdoor air. The economizer operates when outdoor dry-bulb conditions can cool the condenser water to a temperature that can support partially or fully the cooling of the data

Normal Chiller Plant Operation (condenser water temperature above coil design temperature)

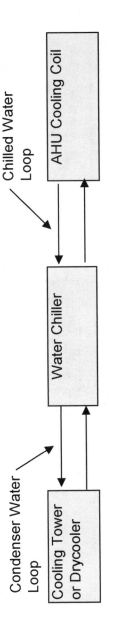

Direct water-side economizer Operation (Condenser water temperature below coil design temperature)

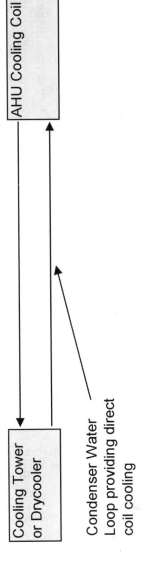

Figure 14.1 Direct water-side economizer.

Normal Chiller Plant Operation (condenser water temperature above coil design temperature)

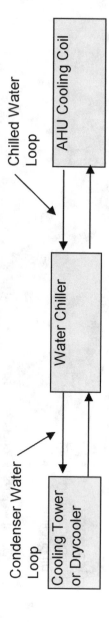

Direct water-side economizer Operation (Condenser water temperature below coil design temperature) (Series arrangement shown in this diagram, allowing for partial economizer operation as a pre-cooler)

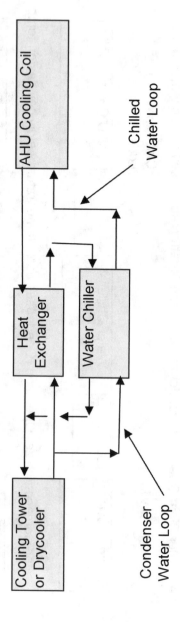

Figure 14.2 Indirect water-side economizer.

center. The cool condenser water is then passed directly through the cooling coil in the computer room air-conditioning unit (CRAC) that absorbs heat from the facility. A more efficient version of this system, allowing more free cooling hours, uses a closed-circuit fluid cooler that improves the heat transfer by spraying water over the heat transfer surface (wet cooler).

14.8 AIR-SIDE ECONOMIZERS

An air-side economizer is an air-handling system that has been designed to use outdoor air for cooling—partially or fully—when the outdoor conditions meet certain criteria. Air dampers are used to adjust the mixture of outdoor air and return air. Sensible economizers use temperature sensors to control the dampers, whereas enthalpy economizers use a combination of temperature and humidity sensors. Figure 14.3 shows the operation of an air-side economizer. When the economizer is not in operation, the return air will mostly be returned rather than exhausted.

During periods of elevated outdoor humidity, sensible economizers (which control the intake of outdoor air based solely on a comparison of the sensible temperature of the return and outside airstreams) have the capacity to admit humid outdoor air. This may be costly in dehumidified facilities and potentially harmful for electronic equipment in facilities without active dehumidification. Low outdoor humidity levels may be costly in humidified facilities and potentially risky for electronic equipment in facilities without active humidification. Indeed, energy savings with enthalpy economizers (which control the intake of outdoor air based on a comparison of the total heat or enthalpy of the return and outside airstreams) are larger than those with sensible economizers when humidification and dehumidification costs are taken into account. Also, enthalpy economizers always save energy, while sensible economizers may waste energy in certain climates. For these reasons, an enthalpy economizer is generally the best choice for a data center or telecommunications facility. Even installations in the humid climates of the Southeast save energy with this control protocol.

The full benefits of enthalpy economizers, however, depend on accurate calibration and maintenance of the humidity sensors. These sensors require calibration more frequently than temperature sensors. Without adequate maintenance, enthalpy economizers have the potential to waste large amounts of energy due to incorrectly positioned dampers and to negatively affect the environmental conditions in the facility.

Economizer operation saves a significant amount of energy, but energy cost savings may be partially offset by costs associated with monitoring equipment to ensure reliability. There are conflicting views concerning potential problems with the use of higher quantities of outside air. There is little published information concerning the severity of problems that may result, such as increased soiling of equipment by submicron particles or higher levels of gaseous pollutants that enter the building with large volumes of outdoor air. Economizer operation, if not properly

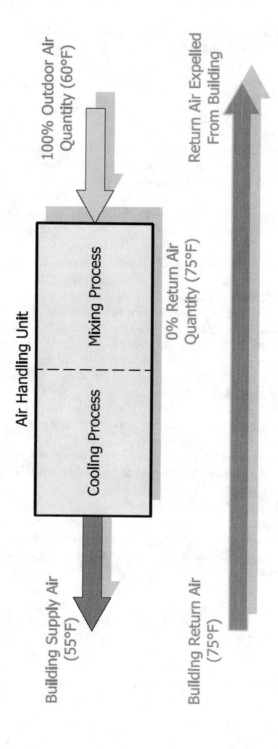

Figure 14.3 Air-side economizer schematic.

controlled, may also result in fluctuating environmental conditions in the facility. Especially of concern are elevated humidity levels that in conjunction with soiled equipment may result in hygroscopic dust failures. Appropriate outdoor air filters are recommended, especially in urban areas.

Air-side economizers are better suited for central station air-handlers than computer room air-handlers (CRAH) that are often used for computer room cooling because the central station air handlers can be located close to outdoor air sources such as exterior walls and roofs.

When evaluating economizers, the reduction in cooling costs should always be compared with the potential added costs associated with maintenance, building space, and equipment reliability problems—true life-cycle cost evaluation. Water-side economizers should be considered in conjunction with air-side economizers. In making an evaluation and comparison, the following points should be taken into consideration:

- There is wide geographic (climatic) variability in the percentage of the year that economizers can be used.
- Some climates are better for water-side economizers and some are better for air-side economizers, depending on ambient humidity levels.
- The percentage utilization of economizers (both water and air side) increases substantially if the data center can operate with a higher supply air temperature.

14.9 OUTDOOR AIR VENTILATION

The primary purpose of outdoor air is to allow for intake of outdoor air for human occupancy and dilution of internally generated pollutants such as volatile organic compounds (VOCs) that can cause electronic equipment failures (Felver 2001). A secondary purpose is to provide positive pressurization of the space to prevent infiltration. Infiltration of hygroscopic dust especially could be a potential cause for premature failure of electronic equipment in conjunction with elevated humidity levels. Infiltration bypasses the filtration systems installed in HVAC equipment, thus increasing dust levels in the facility.

Optimizing use of ventilation air to take advantage of free cooling, yet minimizing it when there are adverse conditions, is an important measure for energy efficency.

Since rates of internal humidity generation are low in a telecom environment (due to the small number of people), the outdoor ventilation rate is the major source of either low (or high) humidity inflow, and this may be the most significant effect of outdoor ventilation rates on the telecom environment. In the winter, any extra outdoor air needs a proportionate amount of humidification added to maintain the desired relative humidity. In the summer, the excess outdoor humidity needs to be taken out of the air.

Telcordia recommends at least 0.25 air exchanges per hour of outdoor air to avoid buildup of indoor airborne pollutants such as VOCs that can harm sensitive electronic equipment (Weschler and Shields 1991).

Telcordia research indicates that there are disadvantages to excessive active pressurization of telecommunications central offices. The outdoor air introduced for the sole purpose of guarding against infiltration generally carries more particles into the building than the added pressure keeps out. To condition this additional air also is associated with an energy premium. Instead of striving for a neutral indoor pressure, however, Telcordia recommends maintaining low controllable pressurization (0.01 in. w.g. [3 Pa]) to avoid unintentional depressurization (Herrlin 1997). The relationship between airflow and space pressurization is examined in chapter 27 of *ASHRAE Fundamentals* (ASHRAE 2005e).

14.10   PART-LOAD OPERATION—GENERATION

Several portions of this chapter have already touched on the issue of trying to maintain energy-efficient cooling system operation at part load. A few additional points that have fallen outside these discussions are listed below.

- **Chiller VFD:** In facilities with central chillers, use of chillers with variable-frequency drives, in the use of multiple staged parallel chillers, is a valid approach to minimizing energy consumption.
- **Compressor Staging:** Many manufacturers provide as an option various methods for variable capacity control. The efficiency of the compressors at low loads is typically better with variable capacity control than with on-off operation, and control is also improved.
- **Pump VFD:** If the pumping system only needs to provide a certain pressure and/or temperature, the use of a VFD on pumps can significantly reduce energy usage. Use of staged multiple parallel pumps in place of a single pump is another approach.
- **Condenser Fan Staging:** Many facilities have multiple condenser fans for cooling purposes. These fans utilize significant energy, and optimization of fan staging as a function of time of year can provide significant energy savings. A trade-off between condenser fan on-time and pump energy and refrigeration system efficiency should be made to optimize energy usage.
- **Condenser Fan VFD:** Installation of variable-frequency drives on condenser fans may be more energy efficient than condenser fan staging.

14.11   IN-ROOM AIRFLOW DISTRIBUTION

Once-through cooling means that the cooling air passes through the electronic equipment only once before returning to the air conditioner. Overcooling and mixing of cold and hot air can be avoided, and the overall thermal efficiency will benefit. The hot-aisle/cold-aisle protocol is currently the favored way of adopting the once-through concept on a global scale in telecom central offices and data centers (Telcordia 2001; ASHRAE, 2004h). The goal is to create cold front aisles and hot rear aisles by supplying cold air into the front aisles and directing hot equipment exhaust toward the rear. The hot-aisle/cold-aisle protocol can be implemented with underfloor, overhead, horizontal displacement or any other method that dependably supplies air into the cold aisles. Blanking panels are essential when an equipment shelf or a complete rack is vacant in a cold-aisle/hot-aisle configuration. The locations of air inlets and exhausts of individual equipment or cabinets are important considerations in achieving high thermal efficiency. The cooling protocol should support the hot-aisle/cold-aisle protocol, which generally means that air needs to be moved from the front to the rear and/or top of the equipment.

The hot-aisle/cold-aisle protocol does not work well with equipment that does not draw air from the front and exhaust to the rear/top. When the number of such racks grows, other cooling protocols must be deployed. Generally, such equipment is best located in a separate area of the equipment room so that the challenges can be treated in isolation and so that other equipment can be arranged in hot and cold aisles. In challenged areas, detailed analyses are often warranted.

14.12 CRAC UNITS—DISTRIBUTION

CRAC units interface with the airflow in a data center by discharging air into a duct or overhead air space, directly into the space, or into a raised-floor air space. Energy efficiency aspects of CRAC unit airflow distribution include the following:

- Efficient distribution of cold air can result in lower overall airflow rates and fan energy usage. Optimization is possible only if one has a thorough understanding of component airflows (servers, cabinets, and CRAC units) and cooling needs. Typically this information must be compiled into a CFD program to build up a model of the facility and perform parametric studies to minimize CRAC unit airflow while maintaining required conditions.
- Fans motors should be specified as premium efficiency.
- Use of VFD drives on CRAC supply fans will lower energy use of the fans—but be alert to the potential for hot spots and some latent cooling at the CRAC cooling coil if flow rates fall too low. One must also be cautious of the potential for freezing a coil at low flow rates with DX units.
- Selection of filters for low pressure drop and regular maintenance of these filters will allow for lower fan energy consumption.
- Placing localized cooling, such as overhead cooling modules, near heat loads will typically allow for a lower fan pressure drop and, thus, reduced distribution energy consumption. The trade-off is lower compressor efficiency.

14.13   PART-LOAD OPERATION—DISTRIBUTION

Data centers and telecommunication facilities typically have the problem that internal loads, apportioned on the basis of watts per unit floor area, are a mix of very high loading and little or no loading. In a telecommunications colocation space, for instance, one suite may be empty, while another may have a load of 150 watts per square foot. As clients change, the reverse may be true in the future. How can a system be designed to handle these significant changes in loads while at the same time maintaining efficient operation?

Many of the standard methods used to achieve energy efficiency at part-load operation in the HVAC industry as a whole are potentially applicable to the design and retrofitting of telecommunications and data center facilities. The concern for the facility designer/operator is to make sure that use of these options does not have an adverse effect on the reliability of the environmental systems or on the ability of the system to serve specific areas with high heat loads. Some of the ideas, as listed in the energy management chapter of the *ASHRAE Handbook—HVAC Applications* (ASHRAE 2003b) and elsewhere (LBNL 2005; PNL 1990), are listed below.

*   **Supply Fan VFD:** At low cooling loads, the speed of the CRAC or other system supply fans can be decreased, saving on fan energy. This option may not be available on all manufacturers' equipment, and the concern exists of maintaining adequate plenum pressurization to provide airflow to specific areas in the space that may have high heat loads. Freezing of coils is also possible with DX units.
*   **Isolating Unused Areas:** In large rooms where the space is clearly underutilized, partitioning the rooms and confining the area to be cooled is another option. This might include shutting off underutilized CRAC units and not installing CRAC units in unpopulated areas until datacom equipment is actually installed. Considerations in taking this approach include the effect of the partition on space (and/or raised-floor air space) pressurization and overall airflow.
*   **Variable Capacity Resources:** A study in 2002 concluded that 25% savings or more can be achieved by designing variable-capacity air-conditioning resources into the data center environment. Strategies that could be employed include use of chilled water, cylinder unloading, and variable-speed drive compressors (Patel 2002). Digital modulation compressors are also available.

14.14   DATACOM EQUIPMENT ENERGY USAGE

Datacom facilities are designed to accommodate IT or telecommunication equipment and provide for their electrical power requirements. Often, the responsibility for the design of the facility and for the specification of the electronic equipment housed in the facility resides in different parts of the owner's organization. Yet to design a center that is as energy efficient as possible, the features of these two areas should be considered together. Any increases in the cost of electronic equipment selected to achieve better efficiency will be offset by reductions in the size of the facility systems and in energy costs, resulting in net savings or very short payback. Studies have shown a wide variation in power supply efficiencies in servers (LBNL 2005). Power supplies are available that can save 20% or more energy relative to inefficient models. These savings not only reduce IT equipment electrical consumption but also create a proportional decrease in cooling load, resulting in additional energy and cost savings. Through a coordinated energy strategy, those responsible for specifying the electronic equipment would be able to require that the electronic equipment have efficient power supplies and easily justify any cost premium through savings in facility capital cost and ongoing operating cost.

Further efficiencies are possible by additional reduction in power conversion losses, idle state power reduction in electronic equipment, processor energy use, fan energy, etc. Redundancy strategies also affect energy efficiency, and a coordinated redundancy strategy should be applied to both the electronic equipment and the facility systems. Specifiers of electronic equipment to be used in datacom facilities need to be aware of its large impact on facility systems and operating cost and their ability to minimize the impact by including energy efficiency as a selection criteria.

For telecommunications central offices, it has been estimated that about 75% of facility energy consumption is related to powering the electronic equipment. Energy efficiency measures at the equipment level would have a cascading effect on most energy-consuming systems in equipment facilities.In 1996, a study identified that for 25% and 50% reductions in telecommunications equipment energy usage, the annual energy cost savings at a typical central office would be approximately $10,000 and $20,000, respectively. These direct savings would be augmented by reduced capital costs of support systems and by the savings associated with increased reliability of electronic equipment. For an estimated 10,000 telephone company central offices across the US, the annual energy savings associated with a 25% reduction would have been about 1,250,000 MWh, valued at $100 million. The introduction of energy-efficient equipment would have provided an unmatched cost-saving potential for telecommunications equipment operators (Herrlin 1996).

The facility designer may not have a great deal of control over the electronic equipment installed in a facility, but, to the extent that there are some options, the energy consumption and environmental specifications of the equipment can have an important impact on the energy use of the facility and on the overall facility budget. The impact of office, computer, and telecommunications equipment on the national energy picture has been estimated from studies in 2002 (Roth et al. 2002; Koomey et al. 2002).

14.15 UPS ENERGY EFFICIENCY

The part-load and full-load energy efficiency of uninterruptible power supply (UPS) modules varies considerably, depending on type of system and model (LBNL

2005). Since all datacom equipment input power typically passes through the UPS during normal operating hours as well as during outages, the energy lost due to a low-efficiency UPS module is significant. Increased UPS efficiency also results in lower cooling load: a 5% increase in UPS efficiency will probably result in a proportional decrease in facility cooling load. As a result, HVAC professionals should work closely with their electrical counterparts to ensure the selection of high-efficiency UPS equipment.

14.16 EMERGING TECHNOLOGIES

Ice storage is a technology that takes advantage of cooling load diversity to make chilled water during off-peak utility billing periods and to use the stored chilled water during the peak billing period. The result is a reduction in the demand charged by the utility for electric power. Telecommunications and data centers tend to have 24/7 operation and reasonably steady power consumption. This tends to make them less attractive to ice storage than facilities with "9-to-5" operation. The reader is referred to Silverling (1995) and Lawson (1988) for computer center designs that make use of this technology. The opportunity to have an emergency cooling source that is independent of chiller operation is more often the driving force.

A technology similar in concept to ice storage is phase-change storage. At least one company markets a phase-change "battery" that can be used in small facilities to eliminate the need for refrigerant-based cooling. The idea is to allow the "battery" to absorb heat in the space during the day and then to discharge it to the atmosphere during the cooler night through use of radiators (Williamson 2001). This technology is not currently intended for either medium or large-scale facilities.

Another new technology is fuel cells, which offer the opportunity for on-site combined heating and power (CHP). A steady load makes a large telecommunications or data center an attractive candidate for CHP. Telecommunications and data centers rarely require space heating due to high internal loads, but the heat from a cogeneration system could be used to run absorption chillers for cooling. A recent *ASHRAE Transactions* article details future opportunities for this emerging technology (Ellis 2002).

Liquid cooling is a technology that promises to lower energy costs. Distribution costs could be substantially lower due to the fact that the volumetric heat capacity of water is about 3500 times the capacity of air at standard conditions (20°C and atmospheric pressure).

14.17 CONTROLS AND ENERGY MANAGEMENT

A significant amount of wasted energy has been found in many existing facilities, often due to fighting between adjacent CRAC units to maintain unnecessarily tight tolerances. Adoption of the somewhat less stringent environmental tolerances found in *Thermal Guidelines for Data Processing Environments* (ASHRAE 2004h) should minimize this problem. Control strategies including networked units and underfloor air temperature control and additional monitoring points should be considered to identify and avoid "fighting" of HVAC systems serving datacom facilities, especially where raised-floor spaces may include a mixture of heat densities in the same open area.

Control systems have long been used as a method of minimizing energy consumption. Most new facilities utilize building automation systems that integrate control and reporting functions. Many of the newer systems are Web-based systems and allow for alarm reporting, automated reports, etc. (Ivanovich 2001).

Since telecommunications and data centers, especially with high heat loads, are energy-intensive, an active energy management program makes good sense. Such a program will make use of an organized approach to identifying and analyzing energy conservation opportunities (ECOs), implementing these measures, and following up with a reporting system to confirm proper implementation and operation. Further information on energy management systems and approaches can be found in the "Energy Use and Management" chapter of the ASHRAE Handbook (ASHRAE 2003b). Concerns about the potential effect of ECOs on overall system reliability must be addressed in the 24/7 operating environment.

14.18 SYSTEM ENERGY SIMULATION

While manual calculations can provide some initial leads as to the most cost-effective environmental system design, computer simulation of the entire facility, including different options for environmental systems, is becoming increasingly popular. The USDOE has a Web site listing energy simulation software applicable to whole buildings (USDOE 2005a) as well as other tools that can be of use to the facility designer (USDOE 2005b). For telecommunications and data center facilities, the system energy simulation analysis is often used in conjunction with a computational fluid dynamics (CFD) model to obtain a full understanding of the facility and to aid in energy optimization.

Simulation of a facility requires very detailed inputs of the equipment in the facility, the peak and part-load efficiency curves of the HVAC equipment, the operational schedule of the facility (typically 24/7 for telecommunications and data centers), and the temperature/humidity setpoint schedule. The details of building construction and outdoor air are also input, and the location of the facility is specified to determine the external variables. Utility rate schedules are usually also input.

Typically, a base model of the facility is run to produce both peak heating and cooling loads and to provide baseline annual energy consumption. Once the baseline is established, specific variables can be changed as discussed above, such as the addition of VFD drives or the addition of an economizer cycle, and the computer makes an alternative run. The output can be used to compare the alternative to the baseline facility. If the cost of the modification is known, the net present value (NPV) of each alternative can be obtained, and cost-effective decisions regarding equipment options and operating setpoints, etc., can be made.

HVAC equipment efficiency is commonly defined by the coefficient of performance. The *ASHRAE Handbook* defines the coefficient of performance for refrigerating cycles as *COP = Useful refrigerating effect/Net energy supplied by external sources* (ASHRAE 2005a). Almost all equipment manufacturers are required to rate their equipment according to either the COP or the EER. The EER, or energy efficiency ratio, is defined as the total cooling output (in British thermal units [Btu]) divided by total energy input (in watt-hours). It is important to understand what auxiliaries are included in the definition. The system energy simulation can make sure that all auxiliary components are accounted for and that the bottom line energy use is obtained.

References and Bibliography

ARI. 1998. *ARI Standard 550/590-98, Standard for Water Chilling Packages Using the Vapor Compression Cycle.* http://www.ari.org/wp/550.590-98wp.pdf.

ASHRAE. 1992. *Standard 52.1-1992, Gravimetric and Dust-Spot Procedures for Testing Air-Cleaning Devices Used in General Ventilation for Removing Particulate Matter.* Atlanta: American Society of Heating, Refrigerating and Air-Conditioning Engineers, Inc.

ASHRAE. 1996. *ASHRAE Guideline 1-1996, The HVAC Commissioning Process.* Atlanta: American Society of Heating, Refrigerating and Air-Conditioning Engineers, Inc.

ASHRAE. 1999. *ANSI/ASHRAE Standard 52.2-1999, Method of Testing General Ventilation Air-Cleaning Devices for Removal Efficiency by Particle Size.* Atlanta:American Society of Heating, Refrigerating and Air-Conditioning Engineers, Inc.

ASHRAE. 2001. *ANSI/ASHRAE Standard 127-2001, Method of testing for rating computer and data processing room unitary air conditioners.* Atlanta: American Society of Heating, Refrigerating and Air-Conditioning Engineers, Inc.

ASHRAE. 2001a. ASHRAE RP-1133, How to verify, validate, and report indoor environmental modeling CFD. Atlanta: American Society of Heating, Refrigerating and Air-Conditioning Engineers, Inc.

ASHRAE. 2003a. *2003 ASHRAE Handbook—HVAC Applications*, chapter 17, Data processing and electronic office areas, Table 1. Atlanta: American Society of Heating, Refrigerating and Air-Conditioning Engineers, Inc.

ASHRAE. 2003b. *2003 ASHRAE Handbook—HVAC Applications*, chapter 35, Energy use and management.

ASHRAE. 2003c. *2003 ASHRAE Handbook—HVAC Applications*, chapter 41, Supervisory control strategies and optimization.

ASHRAE. 2003d. *2003 ASHRAE Handbook—HVAC Applications*, chapter 42, New building commissioning.

ASHRAE 2003e. *2003 ASHRAE—HVAC Handbook Applications*, chapter 47, Sound and vibration control.

ASHRAE. 2003f. *2003 ASHRAE Handbook—HVAC Applications*, chapter 49, Water treatment.

ASHRAE. 2003g. *2003 ASHRAE Handbook—HVAC Applications*, chapter 54, Seismic and wind restraint design.

ASHRAE. 2003h. Risk Management Guidance for Health, Safety and Environmental Security Under Extraordinary Incidents. Atlanta: American Society of Heating, Refrigerating and Air-Conditioning Engineers, Inc.

ASHRAE. 2004a. *2004 ASHRAE Handbook—HVAC Systems and Equipment*, chapter 12, Hydronic heating and cooling system design. Atlanta: American Society of Heating, Refrigerating and Air-Conditioning Engineers, Inc.

ASHRAE. 2004b. *2004 ASHRAE Handbook—HVAC Systems and Equipment*, chapter 13, Condenser water systems.

ASHRAE. 2004c. *2004 ASHRAE Handbook—HVAC Systems and Equipment*, chapter 18, Fans.

ASHRAE. 2004d. *2004 ASHRAE Handbook—HVAC Systems and Equipment*, chapter 20, Humidifiers.

ASHRAE. 2004e. *2004 ASHRAE Handbook—HVAC Systems and Equipment*, chapter 21, Air-cooling and dehumidifying coils.

ASHRAE. 2004f. *2004 ASHRAE Handbook—HVAC Systems and Equipment*, chapter 38, Liquid chilling systems.

ASHRAE. 2004g. *2004 ASHRAE Handbook—HVAC Systems and Equipment*, chapter 39, Centrifugal pumps.

ASHRAE. 2004h. *Thermal Guidelines for Data Processing Environments*. Atlanta: American Society of Heating, Refrigerating and Air-Conditioning Engineers, Inc.

ASHRAE. 2004i. *ANSI/ASHRAE/IESNA Standard 90.1-2004, Energy Standard for Buildings Except Low-Rise Residential Buildings*. Atlanta: American Society of Heating, Refrigerating and Air-Conditioning Engineers, Inc.

ASHRAE. 2004j. *ANSI/ASHRAE Standard 62.1-2004, Ventilation for Acceptable Indoor Air Quality*. Atlanta: American Society of Heating, Refrigerating and Air-Conditioning Engineers, Inc.

ASHRAE. 2005a. *2005 ASHRAE Handbook—Fundamentals*, chapter 1, Thermodynamics and refrigeration cycles. Atlanta: American Society of Heating, Refrigerating and Air-Conditioning Engineers, Inc.

ASHRAE. 2005b. *2005 ASHRAE Handbook—Fundamentals*, chapter 2, Fluid flow.

ASHRAE. 2005c. *2005 ASHRAE Handbook—Fundamentals*, chapter 7, Sound and vibration.

ASHRAE. 2005d. *2005 ASHRAE Handbook—Fundamentals*, chapter 25, Thermal and water vapor transmission data.

ASHRAE, 2005e. *2005 ASHRAE Handbook—Fundamentals*, chapter 27, Ventilation and Infiltration.

ASHRAE. 2005f. *2005 ASHRAE Handbook—Fundamentals*, chapter 30, Nonresidential cooling and heating load calculation procedures.

ASHRAE. 2005g. *2005 ASHRAE Handbook—Fundamentals*, chapter 31, Fenestration.

ASHRAE. 2005h. *2005 ASHRAE Handbook—Fundamentals*, chapter 34, Indoor environmental modeling.

ASHRAE. 2005i. *Datacom Equipment Power Trends and Applications*. Atlanta: American Society of Heating, Refrigerating and Air-Conditioning Engineers, Inc.

ASHRAE. 2005j. *ASHRAE Guideline 0-2005, The Commissioning Process*. Atlanta: American Society of Heating, Refrigerating and Air-Conditioning Engineers, Inc.

ASTM. 1997. *ASTM E 814, Standard Method of Fire Tests of Through-Penetration Fire Stops*. West Conshohocken, PA: American Society for Testing and Materials.

ASTM. 1999. *ASTM E 136, Standard Test Method for Behavior of Materials in a Vertical Tube Furnace at 750°C*. West Conshohocken, PA: American Society for Testing and Materials.

ASTM. 2003. *C 1055-03, Standard Guide for Heated System Surface Conditions that Produce Contact Burn Injuries*. West Conshohocken, PA: American Society for Testing and Materials.

Awbi, H.B., and G. Gan. 1994. Prediction of airflow and thermal comfort in offices. *ASHRAE Journal* 36(2):17–21.

Bash, C.E., C.D. Patel, and R.K. Sharma. 2003. Efficient thermal management of data centers—Immediate and long-term research needs. *HVAC&R Research* 9(2):137–152.

Beaty, D.L. 2004. Liquid cooling—Friend or foe. *ASHRAE Transactions* 110(2):643–652.

Beaty, D.L, and R. Schmidt. 2004. Back to the future: Liquid cooling data center considerations. *ASHRAE Journal* 46(12):42–48.

Beaty, D.L. 2005. Reliability engineering for datacom cooling systems. *ASHRAE Transactions* 111(1):945–953.

Brill, K., E. Orchowski, and L. Strong. 2002. *Product Certification for Fault-Tolerance Is Essential for Verification of High Availability*. The Uptime Institute.

Berglund, B., T. Lindvall, and D.H. Schwela. 1999. *Guidelines for Community Noise*. Geneva: World Health Organization (available at http://www.who.int/docstore/peh/noise/guidelines2).

Cinato, P., et al. 1998. An innovative approach to the environmental system design for TLC rooms in Telecom Italia. *INTELEC 1998*.

Concha-Barrientos, M., D. Campbell-Lendrum, and K. Steenland. 2004. *Occupational Noise: Assessing the Burden of Disease from Work-Related Hearing Impairment at National and Local Levels*. World Health Organization [ISBN 92 4 159192 7] (available at http://www.who.int/quantifying_ehimpacts/publications/9241591927/en/).

Conner, M.C, and L. Hannauer. 1988. Computer center design. *ASHRAE Journal*, April, pp. 20-27.

ECMA. 2003. *Standard ECMA-74, Measurement of Airborne Noise Emitted by Information Technology and Telecommunications Equipment*, 8th ed. (December 2003) ECMA International. http://www.ecma-international.org/publications/standards/Ecma-074.htm

EIA. 1992. EIA-310, revision D, Sept. 1, 1992: Racks, panels and associated equipment. Arlington, VA: Electronic Industries Alliance.

Ellis, M. 2002. Status of fuel cell systems for combined heat and power applications in buildings. *ASHRAE Transactions* 108(1):1032–1044.

EPA. 1990. Clean Air Act amendment. US Environmental Protection Agency. http://www.epa.gov/air/oaq_caa.html/.

Eto, J.H., and C. Meyer. 1988. The HVAC costs of fresh air ventilation. *ASHRAE Journal*, September, pp. 31–35.

ETSI. 1997. *Standard ETS 300 753, Acoustic Noise Emitted by Telecommunications Equipment.* European Telecommunication Standards Institute, 1997 October 01. (available at http://webapp.etsi.org/workprogram/Report_WorkItem.asp?WKI_ID=3392).

ETSI. 2004. *EN 300 019-1-3 V2.2.2, Environmental Conditions and Environmental Tests for Telecommunications Equipment*, Part 1-3: Classification of Environmental Conditions, Stationary Use at Weatherprotected Locations, July. European Telecommunication Standards Institute.

European Union. 2003. EU Directive 2003/10/EC of the European Parliament and of the Council of 6 February 2003 on the minimum health and safety requirements regarding the exposure of workers to the risks arising from physical agents (noise). Available at http://europa.eu.int/eur-lex/pri/en/oj/dat/2003/l_042/l_04220030215en00380044.pdf].

Felver, T.G., M. Scofield, and K. Dunnavant. 2001. Cooling California's computer centers. *HPAC Heating, Piping, Air Conditioning Engineering* 73(3):59–63 (March).

Frank, W.W. 1994. Control of the environment in electrical equipment rooms in the metals industry. *IEEE Transactions on Industry Applications* 30(6):1456–1461 (November/December).

Frey, R.A., B.D. Notohardjono, and R. Sullivan. 2000. Earthquake simulation tests on server computers. PVP, 402(2):1–8.

Griner, J. 1994. What the HEPA can and cannot do. *Cleanrooms*, July.

Harris, C.M., ed. 1994. *Noise Control in Buildings.* New York: Wiley.

Herrlin, M.K. 1996. Economic benefits of energy savings associated with (1) energy-efficient telecommunications equipment and (2) appropriate environmental controls. *Intelec '96, Boston, MA, Oct. 6–10, 1996.*

Herrlin, M.K. 1997. The pressurized telecommunications central office: IAQ and energy consumption. *Healthy Buildings/IAQ '97, Washington DC, Sept. 27-Oct. 2, 1997.*

Herrlin, M.K. 1998. Reduced operating temperature levels in telecommunications huts and vaults: Energy and battery costs. *Intelec '98, San Francisco, CA, Oct. 4-8, 1998.*

Herrlin, M.K. 2005. Rack cooling effectiveness in data centers and telecom central offices: The Rack Cooling Index (RCI). *ASHRAE Transactions* 111(2):725–731.

IBM. 1992. IBM Corporate Bulletin 1-9711-009, Earthquake Resistance for IBM Hardware Products, Guideline for Design and Testing (February).

IBM. 2001. IBM Corporate Standard C-S 1-3705-001, Machine Mobility, Stability, Size and Mass Design Requirements (August).

IEC. 2001. *IEC 60529, Degrees of Protection Provided by Enclosures*, edition 2.1. International Electrotechnical Commission.

IEC. 2002. *60721-3-3. 2002, Classification of groups of environmental parameters and their severities—Stationary use at weather-protected locations.* International Electrotechnical Commission (October).

IEEE. 1990. *IEEE Standard Computer Dictionary: A Compilation of IEEE Standard Computer Glossaries*. New York: Institute of Electrical and Electronics Engineers.

IEEE. 2002a. *IEEE Standard 484, Recommended Practice for Installation Design and Installation of Vented Lead-Acid Storage Batteries for Stationary Applications*. Institute of Electrical and Electronics Engineers.

IEEE. 2002b. *IEEE Standard 1187, Recommended Practice for Installation Design and Installation of Valve-Regulated Lead-Acid Storage Batteries for Stationary Applications*. Institute of Electrical and Electronics Engineers.

IEEE. 2005. Standard 1635, Guide for the Ventilation and Thermal Management of Stationary Battery Installations (draft issue). Institute of Electrical and Electronics Engineers.

ISA. 1985. Document S71.04-1985, *Environmental Conditions for Process Measurement and Control Systems: Airborne Contaminants*. Triangle Park, NC: The Instrumentation, Systems and Automation Society.

ISO. 1985. *ISO 7574, Acoustics—Statistical Methods for Determining and Verifying Stated Noise Emission Values of Machinery and Equipment*, Parts 1, 2, 3 and 4. International Standards Organization.

ISO. 1988. *ISO 9296, Acoustics—Declared Noise Emission Values of Computer and Business Equipment*. International Standards Organization.

ISO. 1999a. *ISO 7779, Acoustics—Measurement of Airborne Noise Emitted By Information Technology And Telecommunications Equipment*, 2d ed. International Standards Organization.

ISO. 1999b. *ISO 14644-1, Cleanrooms and Associated Controlled Environments—Part 1: Classification of Air Cleanliness*. Technical Committee 209 of the International Standards Organization.

ISO. 2000. *ISO 14644-2, Cleanrooms and Associated Controlled Environments—Part 2: Specifications for Testing And Monitoring To Prove Continued Compliance with ISO 14644-1*. Technical Committee 209 of the International Standards Organization.

Ivanovich, M., and S. Arnold. 2001. 20 questions about WACS (Web-accessible control systems) answered. *HPAC Engineering*, April (Part 1), pp. 28–38, and May (Part 2), pp. 59–64.

Jones, D.A. 1992. *Principles and Prevention of Corrosion*. New York: Macmillan Pub. Co.

Kang, S., R.R. Schmidt, K.M. Kelkar, A. Radmehr., and S.V. Patankar. 2001. A methodology for the design of perforated tiles in raised floor data centers using computational flow analysis. *IEEE Transactions on Components and Packaging Technologies*, vol. 24, pp. 177–183.

Karki, K.C., A. Radmehr, and S.V. Patankar. 2003. Use of computational fluid dynamics for calculating flow rates through perforated tiles in raised-floor data centers. *HVAC&R Research* 9(2):153–166.

Kiff, P. 1995. A fresh approach to cooling network equipment. *British Telecommunications Engineering*, July, pp. 149–155.

Koomey, J., et al. 2002. Sorry, wrong number: The use and misuse of numerical facts in analysis and media reporting of energy issues. *Annual Review of Energy and Environment* (also LBNL-50499), vol. 27, pp. 119–158.

Krzyzanowski, M.E., and B.T. Reagor. 1991. Measurement of potential contaminants in data processing environments. *ASHRAE Transactions* 97(1):464–476.

Lawson, S.H. 1988. Computer facility keeps cool with ice storage. *Heating, Piping, Air Conditioning* 60(8):35–38, 43, 44.

LBNL. 2003.Lawrence Berkeley National Laboratories. http://datacenters.lbl.gov/CaseStudies.html.

LBNL. 2005.Lawrence Berkeley National Laboratories. http://hightech.lbl.gov.

Lentz, M.S. 1991. Adiabatic saturation and VAV: A prescription for economy and close environmental control. *ASHRAE Transactions* 97(1):477–485.

Liebert. 2003. Seven Ways Precision Air Conditioning Outperforms Comfort Systems in Controlled Environments. Columbus, OH: Liebert Corp.

Longberg, J.C 1991. Using a central air-handling unit system for environmental control of electronic data processing centers. *ASHRAE Transactions* 97(1):486–493.

Maxcess. 2005. Maxcess Technologies, Inc. Raised access floor specifications. http://www.maxcessfloors.com/home.cfm.

Montgomery, S.W. 2002. Fouling of high density heat sinks—Theoretical origins and numerical analysis. IEEE SEMI-THERM Symposium, August 2002.

Moore, D.A. 2003. The dust threat. IMAPS, October 2003.

Nakao, M., H. Hayama, and M. Nishioka. 1991. Which cooling air supply system is better for a high heat density room: Underfloor or overhead? Thirteenth International Telecommunications Energy Conference (INTELEC '91), November 1991.

Nelson, D. 2003. Auditory demonstrations II: Challenges in speech communication and music listening. NASA Glenn Research Center, available from http://www.grc.nasa.gov/WWW/AcousticalTest/HearingConservation/AuditoryDemonstrations2.htm

NFPA. 1997. *NFPA 12A, Standard on Halon 1301 Fire Extinguishing Systems,* 1997 ed. Quincy, MA: National Fire Protection Association.

NFPA. 1999a. *NFPA 90A, Installation of Air Conditioning and Ventilating Systems,* 1999 ed. Quincy, MA: National Fire Protection Association.

NFPA. 1999b. *NFPA 220, Standard on Types of Building Construction,* 1999 ed. Quincy, MA: National Fire Protection Association.

NFPA. 2000a. *NFPA 12, Standard on Carbon Dioxide Extinguishing Systems,* 2000 ed. Quincy, MA: National Fire Protection Association.

NFPA. 2000b. *NFPA 92A, Recommended Practice for Smoke Control Systems,* 2000 ed. Quincy, MA: National Fire Protection Association.

NFPA. 2000c. *NFPA 92B, Guide for Smoke Control Management Systems in Malls, Atriums and Large Areas,* 2000 ed. Quincy, MA: National Fire Protection Association.

NFPA. 2000d. *NFPA 232, Standard for the Protection of Records,* 2000 ed. Quincy, MA: National Fire Protection Association.

NFPA. 2000e. *NFPA 255, Standard Method of Test of Surface Burning Characteristics of Building Materials,* 2000 ed. Quincy, MA: National Fire Protection Association.

NFPA. 2000f. *NFPA 2001, Standard on Clean Agent Fire Extinguishing Systems,* 2000 ed. Quincy, MA: National Fire Protection Association.

NFPA. 2002a. *NFPA 10, Standard for Portable Fire Extinguishers*, 2002 ed. Quincy, MA: National Fire Protection Association.

NFPA. 2002b. *NFPA 13, Standard for the Installation of Sprinkler Systems*, 2002 ed. Quincy, MA: National Fire Protection Association.

NFPA. 2002c. *NFPA 25, Standard for the Inspection, Testing, and Maintenance of Water-Based Fire Protection Systems*, 2002 ed. Quincy, MA: National Fire Protection Association.

NFPA. 2002d. *NFPA 70, National Electrical Code®*, 2002 ed. Quincy, MA: National Fire Protection Association.

NFPA. 2002e. *NFPA 72®, National Fire Alarm Code®*, 2002 ed. Quincy, MA: National Fire Protection Association.

NFPA. 2002f. *NFPA 76, Recommended Practice for the Fire Protection of Telecommunications Facilities*, 2002 ed. Quincy, MA: National Fire Protection Association.

NFPA. 2003a. *NFPA 14, Standard for the Installation of Standpipe, Private Hydrant, and Hose Systems*, 2003 ed. Quincy, MA: National Fire Protection Association.

NFPA. 2003b. *NFPA 20, Standard for the Installation of Stationary Pumps for Fire Protection*, 2003 ed. Quincy, MA: National Fire Protection Association.

NFPA. 2003c. *NFPA 75, Standard for the Protection of Information Technology Equipment*, 2003 ed. Quincy, MA: National Fire Protection Association.

NFPA. 2003d. *NFPA 101®, Life Safety Code®*, 2003 ed. Quincy, MA: National Fire Protection Association.

NFPA. 2003e. *NFPA 750, Standard for the Installation of Water Mist Fire Protection Systems*, 2003 ed. Quincy, MA: National Fire Protection Association.

NFPA. 2004. *NFPA Standard 70E, Standard for Electrical Safety in the Workplace*. Quincy, MA: National Fire Protection Association.

NFPA. 2005a. *NFPA 11, Low, Medium and High Expansion Foam*, 2005 ed. Quincy, MA: National Fire Protection Association.

NFPA. 2005b. *NFPA Standard 70, National Electric Code®*. Quincy, MA: National Fire Protection Association.

NIOSH. 1986. Occupational Exposure to Hot Environments: Criteria for a Recommended Standard, Revised Criteria, 1986. National Institute for Occupational Safety and Health, Report 86-113. (Also available on the web at: http://www.cdc.gov/niosh/86-113.html.)

Noh, H.-K., K.S. Song, and S.K. Chun. 1998. The cooling characteristics of the air supply and return flow systems in the telecommunication cabinet room. Twentieth International Telecommunications Energy Conference (INTELEC '98), October 1998.

Notohardjono, B.D. 2003. *Tiedown Installation Manual*. IBM manual PN 16R1105, EC J10559, December 22, 2003.

Notohardjono, B.D., J. Wilcoski, and J.B. Gambill. 2004. Design of earthquake resistant server computer structures. *Journal of Pressure Vessel Technology* 126, Issue 1 (February), pp. 66–74.

Osborne, M.W. 1996. Air quality control in control rooms. *IEEE Transactions on Industry Applications* 32(2):443–448.

OSHA. 1996. *29 CFR 1910.95, Occupational Noise Exposure*. U.S. Dept. Labor, Occupational Safety and Health Association, Office of Information, Washington, DC. http://www.osha.gov/pls/oshaweb/owadisp.show_document?p_table =STANDARDS&p_id=9735).

Patanker, S.V., and K. Karki. 2004. Distribution of cooling airflow in a raised-floor data center. *ASHRAE Transactions* 110(2):629–635.

Patel, C.D., C.E. Bash, C. Belady, L. Stahl, and D. Sullivan, 2001. Computational fluids dynamics modeling of high compute density data centers to assure system air inlet specifications, Paper No. IPACK2001-15622. InterPack'01, July 8-13, 2001, Kauai, Hawaii, 2001.

Patel, C.D., R. Sharma, C.E. Bash, and A. Beitelmal. 2002. Thermal considerations in cooling large scale high compute data centers. ITHERM 2002, The Eighth Intersociety Conference on Thermal and Thermomechanical Phenomena in Electronic Systems.

PECI. 1998. *The Model Commissioning Plan and Guide Specifications*, version 2.05. Portland Energy Conservation Inc. http://www.peci.org/library/mcpgs.htm

PNL. 1990. *Architect's and Engineer's Guide to Energy Conservation in Existing Buildings*, vol. 2, chapter 1. DOE/PL/ 01830 P-H4. Pacific Northwest Laboratories.

Proposition 65. 1986. Safe Drinking Water and Toxic Enforcement Act, November. State of California.

Reagor, B.T., and C.A. Russell. 1985. A survey of problems in telecommunication equipment resulting from chemical contamination. *Electrical Contacts 1985 Proceedings of the 31st Meeting of the IEEE Holm Conference on Electric Contact Phenomena, September 29-October 2, 1985*, pp. 157–161.

RMI. 2003. *Energy Efficient Data Centers: A Rocky Mountain Institute Design Charette*. Rocky Mountain Institute.

Rodgers, T. 2005. An owner's perspective on commissioning of critical facilities. *ASHRAE Transactions* 111(2):618–626.

Roth, K., F. Goldstein, and J. Kleinman. 2002. Energy Consumption by Office and Telecommunications Equipment in Commercial Buildings. Volume I: Energy Consumption Baseline. Arthur D. Little Reference No. 72895-00. NTIS Number: PB2002-101438. January.

Schmidt, R., and Cruz, E. 2002. Raised floor computer data center: effect on rack inlet temperatures of chilled air exiting both the hot and cold aisles. *IEEE 2002 Inter Society Conference on Thermal Phenomena*, pp. 580–594.

Schmidt, R. 1997. Thermal management of office data processing centers. InterPack'97, Hawaii.

Schmidt, R. 2001. Effect of data center characteristics on data processing equipment inlet temperatures. Paper No. IPACK2001-15870, InterPack'01, July 8-13, 2001, Kauai, Hawaii.

Schmidt, R.R., K.C. Karki, K.M. Kelkar, A. Radmehr, and S.V. Patankar. 2001. Measurements and predictions of the flow distribution through perforated tiles in raised-floor data centers. Paper No. IPACK2001-15728, InterPack'01, July 8-13, 2001, Kauai, Hawaii.

Shrivastava, S., et al. 2005. Comparative analysis of different data center airflow management configurations. InterPACK 2005, San Francisco, California.

Sorell, V., J. Yang, and S. Escalante. 2005. Comparison of overhead vs. underfloor air distribution in data centers using CFD modeling. *ASHRAE Transactions* 111(2):756–764.

Sharma, R.K., C.E. Bash, and C.D. Patel. 2002. Dimensionless parameters for evaluation of thermal design and performance of large-scale data centers. American Institute of Aeronautics and Astronautics, AIAA-2002-3091.

Silverling, A.M., and K.J. Kressler. 1995. Ice storage system assures data center cooling. *HPAC Heating, Piping, Air Conditioning*, 67(4):35–39.

Stahl, L., and C. Belady. 2001. Designing an alternative to conventional room cooling. International Telecommunications and Energy Conference (INTELEC), Edinburgh, Scotland, October 2001.

SSTS. 2004. *Acoustical Noise Emission of Information Technology Equipment.* Swedish Statskontoret's Technical Standard 26:6, 2004 July 01. (available at http://www.statskontoret.se/upload/2619/TN26-6.pdf.)

Tate. 2005. Tate Access Floor Product Specification. http://www.tateaccess-floors.com/

Telcordia 1994. *GR-1274-CORE, Generic Requirements for Reliability Qualification Testing of Printed Wiring Assemblies Exposed to Airborne Hygroscopic Dust,* Issue 1, May 1994. Piscataway, NJ: Telcordia Technologies, Inc.

Telcordia. 1996. *GR-2930-Core, Network Equipment—Building System (NEBS): Raised Floor Generic Requirement for Network and Data Center.* Piscataway, NJ: Telcordia Technologies, Inc.

Telcordia. 2001. *Generic Requirements NEBS GR-3028-CORE, Thermal Management in Telecommunications Central Offices,* Issue 1, December 2001. Piscataway, NJ: Telcordia Technologies, Inc.

Telcordia. 2002. *GR-63-CORE, Network equipment—Building Systems (NEBS) Requirements: Physical protection. Telcordia Technologies Generic Requirements,* Issue 2, April 2002. Piscataway, NJ: Telcordia Technologies, Inc.

TIA. 2004. *TIA-569-B, Commercial Building Standard for Telecommunications Pathways and Spaces.* Arlington, VA: Telecommunications Industry Association.

TIA. 2005. *TIA 942, Telecommunications Infrastructure Standard for Data Centers.* Telecommunications Industry Association.

Tschudi, B., T. Xu, D. Sartor, and J. Stein. 2003. Roadmap for Public Interest Research for High-Performance Data Centers, LBNL-53483. Lawrence Berkeley National Laboratories.

Turner, W.P., and K. Brill. 2003. Industry Standard Tier Classifications Define Site Infrastructure Performance. The Uptime Institute.

UL. 1980. *UL 478, Standard for Electronic Data-Processing Units and Systems.* Underwriters Laboratories, Inc.

UL. 1994. *UL 900, Standard for Test Performance of Air Filter Units.* Underwriters Laboratories, Inc.

UL. 1995. *UL 1950, Standard for Safety of Information Technology Equipment.* Underwriters Laboratories, Inc.

UL. 2000. *UL 60950, Standard for Safety of Information Technology Equipment.* Underwriters Laboratories, Inc.

UL. 2001a. *UL 60950-1, Standard for Safety of Information Technology Equipment,* 3d ed. Underwriters Laboratories, Inc.

UL. 2001b. *UL 72, Standard for Tests for Fire Resistance of Record Protection Equipment*. Underwriters Laboratories, Inc.

USDOE. 2005a. http://www.eren.doe.gov/buildings/tools_directory/database/page.cfm?Cat=EnergySim&Status=Yes&Menu=1&Sel=1&Desc=Energy+Simulation

USDOE. 2005b. http://www.eren.doe.gov/buildings/tools_directory/database/page.cfm?Menu=7&Desc=Alphabetical+List

USDOL. 1991. *Noise Control: A Guide for Workers and Employers*. U.S. Dept. Labor, Occupational Safety and Health Administration, Office of Information, Washington, DC., 29CFR1910.95, available at http://www.osha.gov/pls/oshaweb/owadisp.show_document?p_table=STANDARDS&p_id=9735

USEPA. 1981. *Noise Effects Handbook, A Desk Reference to Health and Welfare Effects of Noise*. Office of Noise Abatement and Control, U.S. Environmental Protection Agency, October 1979, Revised July 1981. (available at http://www.nonoise.org/library/handbook/handbook.htm.)

Van Dijk, P., and F. van Meijl. 1996. Contact Problems Due to Fretting and Their Solutions. *AMP Journal of Technology* 5(June):14–18. http://www.amp.com/products/technology/5jot_2.pdf.

VanGilder, J., and R. Schmidt. 2005. Airflow uniformity through perforated tiles in a raised-floor data center. InterPACK 2005, San Francisco, California.

Weschler, C.J., and H.C. Shields. 1991. The impact of ventilation and indoor air quality on electronic equipment. *ASHRAE Transactions* 97(1):455–463. Atlanta: American Society of Heating, Refrigerating and Air-Conditioning Engineers, Inc.

Williamson, A.J., et al. 2001. Cooling of telecommunications enclosures in tropical and desert environments. INTELEC 2001, Conf. Pub No. 484, IEEE, Oct 2001.

Wong, C.K., W. Worek, and P. Brillhart. 2002. Use of joint frequency weather data to determine primary energy consumption of desiccant systems. *ASHRAE Transactions* 108(1):608–616. Atlanta: American Society of Heating, Refrigerating and Air-Conditioning Engineers, Inc.

Yamamoto, M., and T. Abe. 1994. The new energy-saving way achieved by changing computer culture (Saving energy by changing the computer room environment). *IEEE Transactions on Power Systems*, vol. 9, August.

Glossary of Terms

absorbed electrolyte: see *electrolyte, absorbed*

ACGIH: American Conference of Governmental Industrial Hygienists

ACH: air changes per hour, typically referring to outdoor air changes per hour

AHU: air-handling unit

air- and liquid-cooled electronics: see *electronics, air- and liquid-cooled*

air- and liquid-cooled rack: see *rack, air- and liquid-cooled*

air- and liquid-cooled server: see *server, air- and liquid-cooled*

air, bypass: air diverted around a cooling coil in a controlled manner for the purpose of avoiding saturated discharge air. On an equipment room scale, bypass air can also refer to the supply air that "short-cycles" around the load and returns to the air handler without producing effective cooling at the load.

air, cabinet: air (typically for the purposes of cooling) that passes through a cabinet housing datacom equipment

air, conditioned: air treated to control its temperature, relative humidity, purity, pressure, and movement

air cooling: see *cooling, air*

air-cooled data center: see *data center, liquid- and air-cooled*

air-cooled electronics: see *electronics, air-cooled*

air-cooled rack: see *rack, air-cooled*

air-cooled server: see *server, air-cooled*

air economizer: see *economizer, air*

air, equipment: airflow that passes through the IT or datacom equipment

air, return (RA): air extracted from a space and totally or partially returned to an air conditioner, furnace, or other heat source

air short-cycling: air conditioners are most efficient when the warmest possible air is returned to them; when cooler-than-expected air is returned to the air conditioner it will perhaps mistakenly read that as the space temperature being satisfied. This air short cycling is because the air is not picking the heat from the space before returning to the air conditioner (see also *air, bypass*).

air space: where the air space below a raised floor or above a suspended ceiling is used to recirculate information technology equipment room/information technology equipment area environmental air, the wiring shall conform to Article 645 of *NFPA 70, National Electrical Code.*

air, supply: air entering a space from an air-conditioning, heating, or ventilating apparatus

aisle, cold: see *hot aisle/cold aisle*

aisle, hot: see *hot aisle/cold aisle*

annunciator: the portion of a fire alarm control panel, or a remote device attached to the fire alarm control panel, that displays the information associated with a notification. Notifications may include alarm or trouble conditions.

ANSI: American National Standards Institute

ASTM International: formerly the American Society for Testing and Materials (ASTM)

availability: a percentage value representing the degree to which a system or component is operational and accessible when required for use

BAS: building automation system

basis-of-design: a document that captures the relevant physical aspects of the facility to achieve the performance requirements in support of the mission (as stated in the Owner's Program document)

battery, VLA: vented lead-acid battery

battery, VRLA: valve regulated lead-acid battery

blanking panels: panels typically placed in unallocated portions of enclosed IT equipment racks to prevent internal recirculation of air from the rear to the front of the rack

BMS: building management system

Btu: abbreviation for British thermal units; the amount of heat required to raise one pound of water one degree Fahrenheit, a common measure of the quantity of heat

building automation system (BAS): centralized building controls typically for the purpose of monitoring and controlling environment, lighting, power, security, fire/life safety, and elevators

bus, electrical: see *bus, power*

bus, power (or electrical bus): a physical electrical interface where many devices share the same electric connection, which allows signals to be transferred between devices, allowing information or power to be shared

bypass air: see *air, bypass*

cabinet: frame for housing electronic equipment that is enclosed by doors and is stand-alone; this is generally found with high-end servers

cabinet air: see *air, cabinet*

CAF: conductive anodic failure

CAV: constant air volume

CFD: computational fluid dynamics

chilled-water system: an air or process conditioning system containing chiller(s), water pump(s), a water piping distribution system, chilled-water cooling coil(s), and associated controls. The refrigerant cycle is contained in a remotely located water chiller. The chiller cools the water, which is pumped through the piping system to the cooling coils.

classes of fires:

   Class A: fires involving ordinary combustibles such as paper, wood, or cloth

   Class B: fires involving burning liquids

   Class C: fires involving any fuel and occurring in or on energized electrical equipment

   Class D: fires involving combustible metals (such as magnesium)

coefficient of performance (COP)—cooling: the ratio of the rate of heat removal to the rate of energy input, in consistent units, for a complete cooling system or factory-assembled equipment, as tested under a nationally recognized standard or designated operating conditions

cold aisle: see *hot aisle/cold aisle*

cold plate: typically, a plate with cooling passages through which liquid flows to remove the heat from the electronic component to which it is attached

commissioning: the process of ensuring that systems are designed, installed, functionally tested, and capable of being operated and maintained to perform in conformity with the design intent; it begins with planning and includes design, construction, start-up, acceptance, and training and can be applied throughout the life of the building

commissioning levels:
    factory acceptance tests (Level 1 commissioning): the testing of products prior to leaving their place of manufacture
    field component verification (Level 2 commissioning): the inspection and verification of products upon receipt
    system construction verification (Level 3 commissioning): field inspections and certifications that components are assembled and properly integrated into systems as required by plans and specifications
    site acceptance testing (Level 4 commissioning): activities that demonstrate that related components, equipment, and ancillaries that make up a defined system operate and function to rated, specified, and/or advertised performance criteria
    integrated systems tests (Level 5 commissioning): the testing of redundant and backup components, systems, and groups of interrelated systems to demonstrate that they respond as predicted to expected and unexpected anomalies

commissioning plan: a document that defines the verification and testing process to ensure the project delivers what is expected, including training, documentation, and project close-out

conditioned air: see *air, conditioned*

cooling, air: conditioned air is supplied to the inlets of the rack/cabinet/server for convective cooling of the heat rejected by the components of the electronic equipment within the rack. It is understood that within the rack, the transport of heat from the actual source component (e.g., CPU) within the rack itself can be either liquid or air based, but the heat rejection media from the rack to the building cooling device outside the rack is air. The use of heat pipes or pumped loops inside a server or rack where the liquid remains is still considered air cooling.

cooling, liquid: conditioned liquid is supplied to the inlets of the rack/cabinet/server for thermal cooling of the heat rejected by the components of the electronic equipment within the rack. It is understood that within the rack, the transport of heat from the actual source component (e.g., CPU) within the rack itself can be either liquid or air based (or any other heat transfer mechanism), but the heat rejection media to the building cooling device outside of the rack is liquid.

COP: coefficient of performance

CPU: central processing unit

CRAC: computer room air-conditioning unit

data center: a building or portion of a building whose primary function is to house a computer room and its support areas; data centers typically contain high-end servers and storage products with mission-critical functions

data center, air-cooled: data center with only air-cooled equipment

data center, liquid- and air-cooled: data center with both chilled air and liquid available

data center, liquid-cooled: data center with only liquid-cooled equipment

datacom: a term that is used as an abbreviation for the data and communications industry

dead-end service rating (valves): valves rated for dead-end service can be placed at the end of a pipe without a cap (i.e., with one end at atmospheric pressure) and will not have any leakage of fluid across the valve at the service pressure rating of the valve

dew-point temperature: see *temperature, dew-point*

dichotomous sampler: piece of measurement equipment that collects airborne particulates and separates them by size for analysis

dielectric fluid: a fluid that is a poor conductor of electricity

direct expansion (DX) system: a system in which the cooling effect is obtained directly from the refrigerant; it typically incorporates a compressor, and in most cases the refrigerant undergoes a change of state in the system

disk unit: hard disk drive installed in a piece of datacom equipment, such as a personal computer, laptop, server, or storage product

diversity: a factor used to determine the load on a power or cooling system based on the actual operating output of the individual equipment rather than the full-load capacity of the equipment

dry-bulb temperature: see *temperature, dry-bulb*

drywell: a well in a piping system that allows a thermometer or other device to be inserted without direct contact with the liquid medium being measured

DX: direct expansion

EC-Class: equipment cooling class

ECM: electronically commutated motor

economizer, air: a ducting arrangement and *automatic* control *system* that allow a cooling supply fan system to supply outdoor (outside) air to reduce or eliminate the need for mechanical refrigeration during mild or cold weather

economizer, water: a system by which the supply air of a cooling system is cooled directly or indirectly or both by evaporation of water or by other appropriate fluid (in order to reduce or eliminate the need for mechanical refrigeration)

EER: energy efficiency ratio

efficiency, HVAC system: the ratio of the useful energy output (at the point of use) to the energy input, in consistent units, for a designated time period, expressed in percent

electrical bus: see *bus, power*

electrolyte: a substance that dissociates free ions when dissolved (or molten) to produce an electrically conductive medium

electrolyte, absorbed: valve regulated lead-acid (VRLA) cells of this design are constructed with a controlled volume of liquid electrolyte contained in a highly absorbent, blotter-like separator positioned between closely spaced plates. This nonwoven separator distributes the electrolyte uniformly and maintains it in contact with the plate active material, while permitting the passage of oxygen evolved during charging. Cells with absorbed electrolyte technology have inherently low internal resistance and can be designed to provide a very high rate, short-duration current. Cells with absorbed electrolyte are also known as "absorbed glass mat" (AGM) types.

electrolyte, gelled: valve regulated lead-acid (VRLA) cells of this design are similar to vented designs, except that the electrolyte has been "gelled" to immobilize it. They can provide a high-rate, short-duration current, but because of the higher internal resistance, they are not as effective as the absorbed electrolyte design. However, the higher thermal conductivity in gelled designs makes them better suited for elevated temperature applications than equivalent absorbed electrolyte cells. A gelled electrolyte cell is typically heavier and larger than an absorbed electrolyte cell for a given capacity.

electromagnetic compatibility (EMC): the ability of electronic equipment or systems to operate in their intended operational environments without causing or suffering unacceptable degradation because of electromagnetic radiation or response

electronically commutated motor (ECM): an EC motor is a DC motor with a shunt characteristic. The rotary motion of the motor is achieved by supplying the power via a switching device—the so-called commutator. On the EC motors, this commutation is performed using brushless electronic semiconductor modules.

electronics, air- and liquid-cooled: electronic equipment that uses both air and liquid

electronics, air-cooled: electronic equipment that is directly cooled by air

electronics, liquid-cooled: electronic equipment that is directly cooled by liquid

electrostatic discharge (ESD): the transfer of voltage between two objects at different voltage potentials

EMC: electromagnetic compatibility

energy efficiency ratio (EER): the ratio of net equipment cooling capacity in Btu/h to total rate of electric input in watts under designated operating conditions. When consistent units are used, this ratio becomes equal to COP (see also *coefficient of performance*)

enthalpy (total heat): see *heat, total*

equipment: refers to, but is not limited to, servers, storage products, workstations, personal computers, and transportable computers; may also be referred to as *electronic equipment* or *IT equipment*

equipment air: see *air, equipment*

ESD: electrostatic discharge

ETSI: European Telecommunications Standards Institute

exchanger, heat: a device to transfer heat between two physically separated fluids *exchanger, rotary heat:* a heat exchanger in which the heat exchange surface rotates

fenestration: an architectural term that refers to the arrangement, proportion, and design of window, skylight, and door systems within a building

filter dryer: encased desiccant, generally inserted in the liquid line of a refrigeration system and sometimes in the suction line, to remove entrained moisture, acids, and other contaminants

float voltage: optimum voltage level at which a battery string gives maximum life and full capacity

gage-cock: a small cock fitted to a pressure or other measurement gage to allow for isolation of the gage for purposes of maintenance

gateway: a hardware or software setup that translates between two dissimilar protocols, or commonly any mechanism for providing access to another system

gelled electrolyte: see *electrolyte, gelled*

global positioning system (GPS): a system of satellites and receiving devices used to compute positions on the Earth

GPS: global positioning system

HDF: hygroscopic dust failure

HDP: horizontal displacement

horizontal displacement (HDP): an air-distribution system used predominantly in telecommunications central offices in Europe and Asia; typically, this system introduces air horizontally from one end of a cold aisle

HVAC system efficiency: see *efficiency, HVAC system*

hygroscopic dust failure (HDF): sulfate and nitrate salts to which water adheres and promotes corrosion

heat exchanger: see *exchanger, heat*

heat exchanger, rotary: see *exchanger, rotary heat*

heat load, latent: cooling load to remove latent heat, where latent heat is a change of enthalpy during a change of state

heat load, sensible: the heat load that causes a change in temperature

heat load per product footprint: calculated by using product measured power divided by the actual area covered by the base of the cabinet or equipment

heat pipe: also defined as a type of heat exchanger; tubular closed chamber containing a fluid in which heating one end of the pipe causes the liquid to vaporize and transfer to the other end where it condenses and dissipates its heat. The liquid that forms flows back toward the hot end by gravity or by means of a capillary wick.

heat, total (enthalpy): a thermodynamic quantity equal to the sum of the internal energy of a system plus the product of the pressure-volume work done on the system:

$$h = E + pv$$

where
h = enthalpy or total heat content,
E = internal energy of the system,
p = pressure, and
v = volume.

For the purposes of this document, h = sensible heat + latent heat.
    sensible heat: heat that causes a change in temperature
    latent heat: change of enthalpy during a change of state

HEPA: high-efficiency particulate air

HFC: hydrofluorocarbon

high-efficiency particulate air (HEPA) filters: These filters are designed to remove 99.97% or more of all airborne pollutants 0.3 microns or larger from the air that passes through the filter. There are different levels of cleanliness, and some HEPA filters are designed for even higher removal efficiencies and/or removal of smaller particles.

HOH: horizontal overhead

horizontal overhead (HOH): an air-distribution system that is used by some long-distance carriers in North America. This system introduces the supply air horizontally above the cold aisles and is generally utilized in raised-floor environments where the raised floor is used for cabling.

hot aisle/cold aisle: a common means of providing cooling to datacom rooms in which IT equipment is arranged in rows and cold supply air is supplied to the cold aisle, pulled through the inlets of the IT equipment, and exhausted to a hot aisle to minimize recirculation of the hot exhaust air with the cold supply air

hot gas: pressurized gas leaving the compressor (discharge) prior to entering the condensing surface *humidity, relative:* see *relative humidity*

hydrofluorocarbon (HFC): a halocarbon that contains only fluorine, carbon, and hydrogen

hydronic: a term pertaining to water used for heating or cooling systems

IEC: International Electrotechnical Commission; a global organization that prepares and publishes international standards for all electrical, electronic, and related technologies.

IEEE: Institute of Electrical and Electronics Engineers

infiltration: flow of outdoor air into a building through cracks and other unintentional openings and through the normal use of exterior doors for entrance and egress; also known as air leakage into a building

iron whiskers: see *whiskers, iron*

ISO: International Organization for Standardization

IT: information technology

ITE: information technology equipment

latent heat load: see *heat load, latent*

leakage airflow: for the purpose of this publication, any airflow that does not flow along an intended path. Leakage airflow results in excess fan energy and may also result in higher energy consumption of refrigeration equipment.

liquid- and air-cooled data center: see *data center, liquid- and air-cooled*

liquid-cooled data center: see *data center, liquid-cooled*

liquid-cooled electronics: see *electronics, liquid-cooled*

liquid-cooled rack: see *rack, liquid-cooled*

liquid-cooled server: see *server, liquid-cooled*

liquid cooling: see *cooling, liquid*

listed: equipment, materials, or services included in a list published by an organization that is acceptable to the authority having jurisdiction and concerned with evaluation of products or services, which maintains periodic inspection of production of listed equipment or materials or periodic evaluation of services, and whose listing states that either the equipment, material, or service meets appropriate designated standards or has been tested and found suitable for a specified purpose (NFPA 2002e).

mainframe: a high-performance computer made for high-volume, processor-intensive computing. This term is used for the processor unit, including main storage, execution circuitry, and peripheral units, usually in a computer center, with extensive capabilities and resources to which other computers may be connected so they can share facilities.

MBH: heat release rate, in units of 1000 British thermal units (Btu) per hour

minimum efficiency reporting value (MERV): previously there were several specifications used to determine filter efficiency and characteristics. ASHRAE has developed the MERV categories so that a single number can be used to select and specify filters.

mean time to repair (or recover) (MTTR): the expected time to recover a system from a failure, usually measured in hours

MERV: minimum efficiency reporting value

MTBF: mean time between failure

MTTR: mean time to repair (or recover)

natural convection overhead (NOH): an air-distribution and cooling strategy in which cooling coils are suspended from the ceiling and air is circulated by natural convection, with no fans or ducting

NEBS™: formerly *network equipment-building system*; provides a set of physical, environmental, and electrical requirements for a central office (CO) of a local exchange carrier (LEC). NEBS is a trademark of Telcordia Technologies, Inc.

NEC: National Electric Code

NFPA: National Fire Protection Association

NIOSH: National Institute for Occupational Safety and Health

NOH: natural convection overhead

OA: outside ventilation air

OSHA: Occupational Safety and Health Administration

Owner's Program: a document that captures the facility's intent (mission) and performance requirements. *ASHRAE Guideline 1-1996* states it is "the document that outlines the owner's overall vision for the facility and expectations of how it will be used and operated" (ASHRAE 1996, p. 2).

pascal (PA): a unit of pressure equal to one newton per square meter. As a unit of sound pressure, one pascal corresponds to a sound pressure level of 94.

PDA: personal digital assistant

PDU: power distribution unit

perforated floor tile: a tile as part of a raised-floor system that is engineered to provide airflow from the cavity underneath the floor to the space, tiles may be with or without volume dampers

personal digital assistant (PDA): a hand-held computer or personal organizer device

plenum: a compartment or chamber to which one or more air ducts are connected and that forms part of the air distribution system (NFPA definition)

power bus (or electrical bus): see *bus, power*

power distribution unit (PDU): the junction point between the UPS and the cabinets containing equipment

psychrometric chart: a graph of the properties (temperature, relative humidity, etc.) of air; it is used to determine how these properties vary as the amount of moisture (water vapor) in the air changes

RA: return air

rack: frame for housing electronic equipment

rack, air- and liquid-cooled: rack that requires both air and liquid provided by the building

rack, air-cooled: an air-cooled rack that accepts ONLY room air

rack, liquid-cooled: a liquid-cooled rack that accepts conditioned coolant

rack-mounted equipment: equipment that is to be mounted in an EIA (Electronic Industry Alliance) or similar cabinet; these systems are generally specified in EIA units, such as 1U, 2U, 3U, etc., where 1U = 1.75 in. (44 mm)

raised floor: a platform with removable panels where equipment is installed, with the intervening space between it and the main building floor used to house the interconnecting cables, which at times is used as a means for supplying conditioned air to the information technology equipment and the room

RC-Class: room-cooling class

redundancy: often expressed compared to the baseline of N, where N represents the number of pieces to satisfy the normal conditions. Some examples are "$N + 1$," "$N + 2$," "$2N$," and "$2(N + 1)$." A critical decision is whether N should represent normal conditions or whether N includes full capacity during off-line routine maintenance. Facility redundancy can apply to an entire site (backup site), systems, or components. IT redundancy can apply to hardware and software.

refrigerants: in a refrigerating system, the medium of heat transfer that picks up heat by evaporating at a low temperature and pressure and gives up heat on condensing at a higher temperature and pressure

relative humidity (RH): (a) ratio of the partial pressure or density of water vapor to the saturation pressure or density, respectively, at the same dry-bulb temperature and barometric pressure of the ambient air; (b) ratio of the mole fraction of water vapor to the mole fraction of water vapor saturated at the same temperature and barometric pressure—at 100% relative humidity, the dry-bulb, wet-bulb, and dew-point temperatures are equal

releasing panel: a particular fire alarm control panel whose specific purpose is to monitor fire detection devices in a given area protected by a suppression system and, upon receiving alarm signals from those devices, actuate the suppression system.

reliability: a percentage value representing the probability that a piece of equipment or system will be operable throughout its mission duration. Values of 99.9% (three 9s) and higher are common in data and communications equipment areas. For individual components, the reliability is often determined through testing. For assemblies and systems, reliability is often the result of a mathematical evaluation based on the reliability of individual components and any redundancy or diversity that may be employed.

remote power panel (RPP): a term typically used to describe electrical panels outside of electrical equipment rooms

return air: see *air, return*

RH: relative humidity

RHI: Return Heat Index

riser: a vertical pipe in a building

rotary heat exchanger: see *exchanger, rotary heat*

rotary UPS: see *UPS, rotary*

RPP: remote power panel

sensible heat load: see *heat load, sensible*

sensible heat ratio (SHR): ratio of the sensible heat load to the total heat load (sensible plus latent)

server: a computer that provides some service for other computers connected to it via a network; the most common example is a file server, which has a local disk and services requests from remote clients to read and write files on that disk

server, air- and liquid- cooled: server that requires both air and liquid provided by the building

server, air-cooled: an air-cooled server that accepts ONLY room air

server, liquid-cooled: a liquid-cooled server that accepts conditioned coolant

service level agreement (SLA): a contract between a network service provider and a customer that specifies, usually in measurable terms, what services the network service provider will furnish

SHR: sensible heat ratio

single-point failure: any component that has the capability of causing failure of a system or a portion of a system if it becomes inoperable.

SLA: service level agreement

static UPS: see *UPS, static*

supply air: see *air, supply*

switchgear: combination of electrical disconnects and/or circuit breakers meant to isolate equipment in or near an electrical substation

telecom: abbreviation for *telecommunications*

temperature, dew-point: the temperature at which water vapor has reached the saturation point (100% relative humidity)

temperature, dry-bulb: the temperature of air indicated by a thermometer.

temperature, wet-bulb: the temperature indicated by a psychrometer when the bulb of one thermometer is covered with a water-saturated wick over which air is caused to flow at approximately 4.5 m/s (900 ft/min) to reach an equilibrium temperature of water evaporating into air, where the heat of vaporization is supplied by the sensible heat of the air

thermal effectiveness: measure of the amount of mixing between hot and cold airstreams before the supply air can enter the equipment and before the equipment discharge air can return to the air-handling unit

thermal efficiency: energy output as a percentage of energy input of a machine or process

thermal storage tank: container used for the storage of thermal energy; thermal storage systems are often used as a component of chilled-water systems

thermosyphon: an arrangement of tubes for assisting circulation in a liquid through the use of capillary action

tin whiskers: see *whiskers, tin*

total heat (enthalpy): see *heat, total*

turn-down ratio: ratio representing highest and lowest effective system capacity. Calculated by dividing the maximum system output by the minimum output at which steady output can be maintained. For example, a 3:1 turn-down ratio indicates that minimum operating capacity is one-third of the maximum.

UPS: uninterruptible power supply

UPS, rotary: a flywheel-driven UPS that is used for applications requiring ride-through of short-duration power system outages, voltage dips, etc. The flywheel-driven rotary UPS typically does not include batteries, and support times are usually on the order of a few seconds to a few minutes.

UPS, static: typically uses batteries as an emergency power source to provide power to datacom facilities until emergency generators come on line

vapor barrier: a material or construction that adequately impedes the transmission of water vapor under specified conditions

VAV: variable air volume

ventilation: the process of supplying or removing air by natural or mechanical means to or from any space; such air may or may not have been conditioned

vertical overhead (VOH) class: refers to the delivery of air from overhead ductwork

vertical underfloor (VUF) class: refers to the delivery of air from an underfloor space, i.e., a raised-floor cavity

VLA battery: see *battery, VLA*

VOC: volatile organic compound

VOH: vertical overhead

volatile organic compounds (VOCs): organic (carbon-containing) compounds that evaporate readily at room temperature; these compounds are used as solvents, degreasers, paints, thinners and fuels

VRLA battery: see *battery, VRLA*

VUF: vertical underfloor

water economizer: see *economizer, water*

wet-bulb temperature: see *temperature, wet-bulb*

whiskers, iron: crystalline metallurigical phenomenon whereby iron grows tiny hairs, which can become airborne under certain conditions and settle in electronic equipment

whiskers, tin: a crystalline metallurigical phenomenon whereby tin grows tiny hairs, which can become airborne under certain conditions and settle in electronic equipment

whiskers, zinc: a crystalline metallurigical phenomenon whereby zinc grows tiny hairs, which can become airborne under certain conditions and settle in electronic equipment

zinc whiskers: see *whiskers, zinc*

Index

A

absorbed electrolyte 65, 169, 174
absorbed glass mat 171, 177
ACGIH 75, 169
ACH 82, 169
acoustical 4, 56–57, 67, 87–92, 94–95
acoustical noise emissions 87
acoustics 3, 87–88
AGM 171, 177
AHU 26, 39, 40, 42–45, 169
air- and liquid-cooled electronics 169, 175
air- and liquid-cooled rack 169, 180
air- and liquid-cooled server 169, 182
air and liquid cooling 47
air, bypass 169, 171
air, cabinet 169, 171
air changes per hour 82, 169
air, conditioned 39, 47, 169, 172
air-cooled/air cooling 16, 18, 24, 26–27, 29–30, 35, 47, 49, 139, 141, 169, 172
air-cooled data center 169, 173
air-cooled datacom equipment 87
air-cooled electronics 35, 169, 175
air-cooled rack 49, 53–55, 169, 180
air-cooled server 169, 182
air distribution 2–4, 26, 35, 41–42, 45–46, 63, 98
air economizer 45, 82, 137, 149–51, 170, 174
air, equipment 63, 170, 175
airflow, equipment 3, 36–37
airflow, leakage 40, 42, 178
airflow rate 16, 37, 40, 153
air-handling unit 26, 39, 40, 42–45, 169

HFC 27, 115, 177–78
high density 2, 18–19
high-efficiency particulate air 76, 84, 162, 177
HOH 46, 177
horizontal displacement 46, 153, 176
horizontal overhead 46, 177
hot aisle 3, 15, 36–38, 40, 44, 46, 153, 170, 177
hot gas 24, 142, 177
human comfort 2, 15
human error 4, 84, 135
humidification 14, 21–24, 26, 32, 73–74, 138, 142, 144, 149, 151
humidifier 142
humidity 1–2, 4, 7–9, 13–16, 19, 21–22, 24, 26, 32–35, 61, 67, 70, 72, 80–82, 109, 131–32, 137–39, 144–45, 149, 151, 157, 178
humidity, relative 7–9, 13–16, 21, 32, 35, 70, 72, 81, 138, 144, 151, 178, 181
HVAC load 2, 17
HVAC system efficiency 174, 176
hybrid 53, 54, 55
hybrid system 49
hydrofluorocarbon 27, 115, 177–78
hydrogen chloride 71, 74
hydrogen sulfide 71, 74
hydronic 178
hygroscopic 13, 72, 76, 151
hygroscopic dust failure 13, 151, 176

I

IEC 69, 74, 76, 162, 178
IEEE 63–65, 76, 131, 163, 178
immission 89–90
indoor air quality 14, 75
infiltration 14–15, 19, 78, 144–45, 151–52, 178
information technology 178
information technology equipment 16, 32, 36–37, 46, 69–70, 73–85, 89, 92–94, 132, 136, 155, 173, 178
infrared 24, 32, 109
Institute of Electrical and Electronics Engineers 63–65, 76, 131, 163, 178
Instrumentation, Systems and Automation Society, The 163
insulation 21, 31, 70, 78, 83
integrated systems tests 172
International Electrotechnical Commission 74, 76, 162, 178
International Organization for Standardization 14, 75, 92, 163, 178
intumescent 120
ionization 108
iron whiskers 3, 83, 178, 184
ISA 163

S

supplemental cooling 37, 46
supply air 35–36, 38, 40–46, 65–66, 75, 80, 142, 144, 151, 170, 182
Supply Heat Index 38
suppression abort 110
switchgear 61, 182
system construction verification 172

T

T rating 120
tape storage 19–20
Telcordia Technologies, Inc 3, 8, 69, 74, 168, 182
telecom 182
Telecommunications Industry Association 74, 167
temperature 1–2, 7–9, 12–18, 24, 26, 29–39, 43, 45, 48, 57–58, 61, 63–67, 70, 72, 74, 80–83, 109, 115, 117–20, 131–33, 136, 138–41, 145–46, 149, 151–52, 157, 173–74, 182, 184
temperature, dew-point 8, 173, 182
temperature, dry-bulb 16, 139, 141, 174, 182
temperature, rack 33
temperature rate of change 2, 9, 12, 133
temperature, wet-bulb 16, 139, 141, 146, 182, 184
test lab 67
thermal effectiveness 36–39, 183
thermal efficiency 72–73, 152–53, 183
thermal guidelines 7–18, 22, 33, 38, 57, 67, 69, 80, 138, 156, 160
thermal storage tank 58, 183
thermosyphon 47, 183
TIA 74, 167
tie-down 103–105
tin whiskers 79, 183
total heat 175, 177, 183
transmission 21, 89, 90
turn-down ratio 183

U

ultrasonic 24, 32, 142
ultraviolet 109
underfloor 3, 26, 33, 38–42, 45–46, 79–80, 93, 101, 111, 134, 153, 157, 186–87
uninterruptible power supply 19, 32, 58, 61, 63, 127–28, 137, 155–56, 183
UPS 19, 32, 58, 61, 63, 127–28, 137, 155–56, 183
UPS, rotary 181, 183
UPS, static 128, 182–83

V

valve 26–31, 49, 56, 65, 110, 112, 117–18, 134–36, 139, 143, 145–46
valve regulated lead-acid battery 65, 170, 174, 184